To the Fitzge...

With affection

A Catholic Bill of Rights

From Pat Conan, SVD

a.k.a.

Edited by

Leonard Swidler
Herbert O'Brien

Sheed & Ward

Sheed & Ward™ is a service of National Catholic Reporter Publishing
Company, Inc.

Library of Congress Catalog Card Number: 87-62663

ISBN: 1-55612-098-2

Published by: Sheed & Ward
          115 E. Armour Blvd. P.O. Box 414292
          Kansas City, MO 64141-4292

To order, call: (800) 333-7373

Contents

"Justice in the World" Second Synod of Bishops—1971

III. The Practice of Justice
The Church's Witness

39. Many Christians are drawn to give authentic witness on behalf of justice by various modes of action for justice, action inspired by love in accordance with the grace which they have received from God. For some of them, this action finds its place in the sphere of social and political conflicts in which Christians bear witness to the Gospel by pointing out that in history there are sources of progress other than conflict, namely love and right. This priority of love in history draws other Christians to prefer the way of non-violent action and work in the area of public opinion.

40. While the Church is bound to give witness to justice, she recognizes that anyone who ventures to speak to people about justice must first be just in their eyes. Hence we must undertake an examination of the modes of acting and of the possessions and life style found within the Church herself.

41. Within the Church rights must be preserved. No one should be deprived of his ordinary rights because he is associated with the Church in one way or another. Those who serve the Church by their labour, including priests and religious, should receive a sufficient livelihood and enjoy that social security which is customary in their region. Lay people should be given fair wages and a system for promotion. We reiterate the recommendations that lay people should exercise more important functions with regard to Church property and should share in its administration.

42. We also urge that women should have their own share of responsibility and participation in the community life of society and likewise of the Church.

43. We propose that this matter be subjected to a serious study employing adequate means: for instance, a mixed commission of men and women, religious and lay people, of differing situations and competence.

44. The Church recognizes everyone's right to suitable freedom of expression and thought. This includes the right of everyone to be heard in a spirit of dialogue which preserves a legitimate diversity within the Church.

45. The form of judicial procedure should give the accused the right to know his accusers and also the right to a proper defence. To be complete, justice should include speed in its procedure. This is especially necessary in marriage cases.

46. Finally, the members of the Church should have some share in the drawing up of decisions, in accordance with the rules given by the Second Vatican Ecumenical Council and the Holy See, for instance with regard to setting up of councils at all levels.

Introduction

Leonard Swidler & Herbert O'Brien[1]

In a famous peroration to a sermon on "A Changing Church—to the baffled and hurt," Walter Burghardt, SJ, said: "Let me make an uncommonly honest confession. In the course of half a century I have seen more Catholic corruption than you have read of. I have tasted it. I have been reasonably corrupt myself. And yet, I joy in this Church—this living, pulsing, sinning people of God, love it with a crucifying passion. Why? For all the Catholic hate, I experience here a community of *love*. For all the institutional idiocy, I find here a tradition of *reason*. For all the individual repressions, I breathe here an air of *freedom*. For all the fear of sex, I discover here the redemption of my *body*. In an age so inhuman, I touch here tears of *compassion*. In a world so grim and humorless, I share here rich *joy* and earthy *laughter*. In the midst of death, I hear here an incomparable stress on *life*. For all the apparent absence of God, I sense here the real presence of *Christ*."

The Council Fathers at Vatican II put it more tersely: they said that while the Church is holy, it is also a Church "semper reformanda"—i.e., a sinful Church that must always be reforming itself, always being converted from sin. These twin aspects of the Church, its holiness and its sinfulness, provide the background to this book of essays on the rights of Catholics in the Church.

For, on the one hand, there are many good things said about the rights of Catholics in the Code of Canon Law, e.g., Canon 221 states that "the Christian faithful can legitimately vindicate and defend the rights which they enjoy in the Church before a competent ecclesiastical court, in accord with the norm of law." And, as James Coriden points out in his introductory essay, "Making the Rights Real," John Paul II singled out the Code's Charter of Rights for special attention just after the promulgation of the Code. Indeed, in promulgating the new Code he said that "the rights of individuals" must be "guaranteed and well-defined."

The other side of the coin is, however, that although the Code makes explicit many rights that Catholics have, e.g. "the right to advise pastors regarding the good of the Church, and to participate in public opinion and in informing the faithful "(C. 212, 3), the experience of the People of God is that the rights of Catholics are often violated, not only in the rarefied world of theology, where theologians are condemned by "Rome" without having a chance to confront their accusers, and in the higher realms of Church politics, where archbishops are stripped of their administrative powers, without due process, but at the parish level, where most Catholics experience the Church. For example, a pastor may spend his parishioners' money without any sort of accountability, let alone prior consultation; a parish employee, like a DRE, may be dismissed without just cause or due process; schools may be closed without the authorities' consulting the parents of the children involved.

It is the contention of the Association for the Rights of Catholics in the Church (ARCC) that there are some rights that are not in the Code which should be there—e.g., the right of the faithful to have a say in who their pastors will be; the right to financial accountability; the right to practice that form of family-planning (outside of abortion) that a couple in conscience find most suitable for them, etc., etc. It was because of this feature of the Code—the missing rights—that ARCC in 1983 published a more comprehensive *Charter of the Rights of Catholics in the Church*. This Charter was the result of prolonged and wide consultation among Catholics not only in the United States but also abroad. The Charter has been translated into French, Dutch, Spanish, Polish, German and Italian. One note about the Charter: after each right, there is a reference to the relevant canon or canons that treat *in some way* of the particular right (see Appendix I). ARCC does not claim that in every case the Code supports the rights in the Charter. Sometimes the opposite is the case. ARCC sanguinely looks forward to the day when this Charter will be incorporated into official Church statutes. One modest step towards this goal is this book: *A Catholic Bill of Rights*.

The editors asked the authors to each write an essay on a particular right. The general aim was to provide, in a short essay (Eric Hoffer of the University of California at Berkeley once said: "There is not an idea that cannot be expressed in 200 words"—and we tend to agree with him), the theological and/or philosophical foundation for each right. Some authors have preferred to give their own reflection on a right. The editors regret that the male authors outnumber the females. All attempts to achieve a balance failed. ARCC hopes that the book will stimulate further discussion about the rights of Catholics.

A few words about the history of ARCC: In February, 1980, in the wake of the Vatican's withdrawing from Hans Küng his right to be known as a Roman Catholic theologian, a group of American Catholics, both lay and clerical, from ten metropolitan areas of the United States, met in Milwaukee to discuss what might be done about the cases of Edward Schillebeeckx, Jacques Pohier and Hans Küng, theologians whose Catholic credentials had been impugned by Rome, and how to prevent such things from happening in the future.

Not far from the minds of the concerned Catholics meeting in Milwaukee was the statement of the 1971 Synod of Bishops: "While the Church is bound to give witness to justice, she recognizes that anyone who ventures to speak to people about justice must first be just in their eyes. Hence we must undertake an examination of the modes of acting and of the possessions and life-style found within the Church itself. *Within the Church, rights must be preserved.*" To help achieve this goal of a just Church, the Association for the Rights of Catholics in the Church was founded. It now numbers about 1000 members in the United States, and liaises with similar groups in Poland, West Germany, Belgium, Holland, Australia and France. Formally set out, ARCC's goal is: "to bring about substantive structural change in the Church. It seeks to institutionalize a collegial understanding of Church in which decision-making is shared and accountability is realized among Catholics of every kind and condition. It affirms that there are fundamental rights which are rooted in the humanity and baptism of all Catholics."[2]

Canon 208 of the Code of Canon Law says: "There exists among all the Christian faithful, in virtue of their rebirth in Christ, a true equality." This book tries to make explicit some of the implications of that landmark statement, implications which, ARCC hopes, will one day become an accepted part of the ever-vibrant life of our beloved Church, Father Burghardt's "living, pulsing, sinning people of God."

The editors wish to thank Kathy Ott and Christine Etsell for their untiring labors in preparing the essays for publication.

Notes

1. A pseudonym.

2. For more information about ARCC write to P.O. Box 912, Delran, NJ 08075. Phone 609-764-9266.

Charter of the Rights of Catholics in the Church

Preamble

The rights of Catholics in the Church derive both from our basic humanity as persons and from our baptism as Christians. Membership in the human community and membership in the community of the Church, therefore, jointly confer the rights here presented which guarantee our dignity and freedom as persons and as Catholics.

Fundamental rights are clearly set forth in the United Nations Charter (see Appendix II). This Charter of the Rights of Catholics in the Church presupposes the rights expressed in the U.N. Charter. These basic human rights are supplemented by the common rights and freedom of Christians bestowed at baptism, and based on: (1) the universal priesthood of all believers, (2) the fundamental equality of believers, and (3) the prophetic role of all believers.

Moreover, Vatican Council II urged the Church to read and learn from "the signs of the times." One of the clear signs of the times in many countries is a concern for human rights.

The framers of this Charter of Rights for Catholics maintain that faithfulness to the message of the Gospel mandates a concern for justice in the Church, as well as in the world. The Church, by its very nature, must labor for the liberation of those oppressed and marginalized by sinful social structures, which often make it impossible for many men and women to claim even their basic human rights. The Church as a

People of God, and not individual Christians only, is called to give witness to the love commandment. This responsibility entails, especially, the renewal of the Church's own structural organization where it is seen to foster injustice and to deny to some Catholics the rights of persons and the freedom of Christians. "Justice is love's absolute minimum" (Paul VI). The institutional Church, as a human society, can therefore no longer justify an authoritarian and partriarchial order appropriate to earlier stages of human development. The Social Justice teachings of the Church, especially as set forth in Paul VI's "Populorum Progressio," are presupposed by this Charter.

Fundamental to this Charter is the principle that all Catholics are radically equal. Canon 208 of the revised Code of Canon law states: "There exists among all the Christian faithful, in virtue of their rebirth in Christ, a true equality with regard to dignity and activity; all cooperate in the building up of the body of Christ in accord with each one's own condition and function." In other words, the equality of all Catholics is based on their one Lord, one faith, one call and one common sacramental initiation. Therefore, rights and equality are not diminished by differing gifts and roles of Church members. Christ has destroyed all divisions, "between Jew and gentile, male and female, slave and free" (Gal. 3:28). Thus, because all are equally beloved by God, each one's ability to respond to that God and to actualize his or her capacities within the Church community, must not be limited by consideration of race, age, nationality, sex, sexual orientation, state-of-life or social position.

The revised Code of Canon Law (see Appendix I) only partially articulates the principles which should inform a just, loving, and therefore fruitful relationship between the magisterium and the People of God.

Rights do not exist in isolation, but rather only in conjunction with corresponding responsibilities. But it is vital to remember that no responsibilities can be properly carried out without the safeguarding and exercising of those human and Catholic rights.

In view of these considerations, there is, then, a need for a clear and complete Charter of the rights of Catholics in the Church, rights that are founded on (and limited by) the Gospel and on the authentic tradition of the Church.

This Charter, therefore, proclaims the following Catholic rights.

Basic Rights

1. All Catholics have the right to follow their informed consciences in all matters. (Canon 748.1)

2. Officers of the Church have the right to teach on matters both of private and public morality only after wide consultation prior to the formulation of their teaching. (C. 212, C. 747, C. 749, C. 752, C. 774.1)

3. All Catholics have the right to engage in any activity which does not infringe on the rights of others, e.g., they have the right to freedom of speech, freedom of the press, and freedon of association. (C. 212:2,3, C. 215, C. 223:1)

4. All Catholics have the right of access to all information possessed by Church authorities concerning their spiritual and temporal welfare, provided such access does not infringe on the rights of other. (C. 218, C. 221:1,2,3, C. 223:1, C. 537)

Decision-Making and Dissent

5. All Catholics have the right to a voice in all decisions that affect them, including the choosing of their leaders. (C. 212:3)

6. All Catholics have the right to have their leaders accountable to them. (C. 492, C. 1287.2)

7. All Catholics have the right to form voluntary associations to pursue Catholic aims including the right to worship together; such associations have the right to decide on their own rules of governance. (C. 215, C. 299, C. 300, C. 305, C. 309)

8. All Catholics have the right to express publicly their dissent in regard to decisions made by Church authorities. (C. 212:3, C. 218, C. 753)

Due Process

9. All Catholics have the right to be dealt with according to commonly accepted norms of fair administrative and judicial procedures without undue delay. (C. 221:1,2,3, C. 223,1,2)

10. All Catholics have the right to redress of grievances through regular procedures of law. (C. 221:1,2,3, C. 223:1,2)

11. All Catholics have the right not to have their good reputations impugned or their privacy violated. (C. 220)

Ministries and Spirituality

12. All Catholics have the right to receive from the church those ministries which are needed for the living of a fully Christian life, including:

a) Instruction in the Catholic tradition and the presentation of moral teaching in a way that promotes the helpfulness and relevance of Christian values to contemporary life. (C. 229:1,2)

b) Worship which reflects the joys and concerns of the gathered community and instructs and inspires it.

c) Pastoral counseling that applies with love and effectiveness the Christian heritage to persons in particular situations. (C. 213, C. 217)

13. All Catholics have the right, while being mindful of Gospel norms, to follow whatever paths will enhance their life in Christ (i.e., their self-realization as unique human beings created by God). They also have the right to guidance that will foster authentic human living both on a personal level and in relation to their communities and the world. (C. 213)

14. All Catholics have the right to follow the customs and laws of the rite of their choice and to worship accordingly. (C. 214)

15. All Catholics, regardless of race, age, nationality, sex, sexual orientation, state-of-life, or social position have the right to receive all the sacraments for which they are adequately prepared. (C. 213, C. 843:1)

16. All Catholics, regardless of canonical status (lay or clerical), sex or sexual orientation, have the right to exercise all ministries in the Church for which they are adequately prepared, according to the needs and with the approval of the community. (C. 225:1, C. 274:1, C. 1024)

17. All Catholics have the right to have Church office-holders foster a sense of community. (C. 369, C. 515)

18. Office-holders in the Church have the right to proper training and fair financial support for the exercise of their offices, as well as the requisite respect and liberty needed for the proper exercise thereof. (C. 231:2, C. 281)

19. All Catholics have the right to expect all office-holders in the Church to be properly trained and to continue their education throughout their term of office. (C. 217, C. 231:1, C. 232, C. 279, C. 819)

20. Catholic teachers of theology have a right to responsible academic freedom. The acceptability of their teaching is to be judged in dialogue with their peers, keeping in mind the legitimacy of responsible dissent and pluralism of belief. (C. 212:1, C. 218, C. 750, C. 752, C. 754, C. 279:1, C. 810, C. 812)

Social and Cultural Rights

21. All Catholics have the right to freedom in political matters. (C. 227)

22. All Catholics have the right to follow their informed consciences in working for justice and peace in the world. (C. 225:2)

23. All employees of the Church have the right to decent working conditions and just wages. They also have the right not to have their employment terminated without due process. (C. 231:2)

24. All Catholics have the right to exercise their artistic and cultural talents without interference (e.g., censorship) from Church authorities; likewise all Catholics have the right freely to enjoy the fruits of the arts and culture.

States of Life

25. All Catholics have the right to choose their state in life; this includes the right to marry and the right to embrace celibacy.

26. All Catholic women have an equal right with men to the resources and the exercise of all the powers of the Church.

27. All Catholics have the right to expect that the resources of the Church be fairly expended on their behalf without prejudice to race, age, nationality, sex, sexual orientation, state-of-life, or social position.

   a) All Catholic parents have the right to expect fair material and other assistance from Church authorities in the religious education of their children.

   b) All single Catholics have the right to expect that the resources of the Church be fairly expended on their behalf.

28. All married Catholics have the right to determine in conscience the size of their families and the appropriate methods of family planning.

29. All Catholic parents have the right to see to the education of their children in all areas of life. (C. 226:2)

30. All married Catholics have the right to withdraw from a marriage which has irretrievably broken down. All such Catholics retain the radical right to remarry.

31. All Catholics who are divorced and remarried and who are in conscience reconciled to the Church have the right to the same ministries, including all sacraments, as do other Catholics.

Language

32. All Catholics have the right to expect that Church documents and materials will avoid sexist language and that symbols and imagery of God will not be exclusively masculine.

A Challenge: Making the Rights Real[1]

James A. Coriden

A rugged monument to President Lyndon Johnson stands on the west bank of the Potomac river at Washington. It is a simple, rough-hewn shaft of granite set in a grove of trees. On its base are inscribed the words Johnson spoke on January 14, 1969, at the end of his term of office:

> I hope it may be said, a hundred years from now, that by working together we helped to make our country more just for all its people . . . I believe at least it will be said that we tried.

He referred to the difficult struggle to enact and then enforce the Civil Rights Act of 1964.

The Code of 1983 presents canonists with a similar challenge: to make our church more just for all its members. The Code contains a list of rights and obligations. Thus far they remain mere statements, unrealized in the life of the church. Can we make them real? Will it be said that at least we tried?[2]

The challenge to make the rights real unfolds here as follows:

James Coriden is a priest of the diocese of Gary, Indiana and is Academic Dean at Washington Theological Union, where he teaches Canon Law. He is on ARCC's Board of Directors.

1. our church is frequently perceived as unfair or arbitrary, especially in the way members suffer at the hands of leaders;

2. the 1983 Code proffers a "Bill of Rights" for members which is of constitutional status;

3. our tradition demands that we take rights seriously: evidence arises from, a) the New Testament, b) the medieval canonists, and c) the modern teaching on human rights;

4. a theoretical corollary is found in the contemporary debate about rights in any society;

5. practical proposals proceed along two lines: tribunals and alternatives.

1. AN UNJUST CHURCH

The Roman Catholic Church labors under a popular perception that it is arbitrary and unjust. The kinds of actions and failings which create and verify that image are the everyday and commonplace things which befall ordinary faithful and their parishes. Grander injustices and more spectacular abuses at high levels serve to reinforce this image of an authoritarian and unfair church. But the real damage is done at the local level. The denials of rights, non-feasance of office and capricious behavior which affect the ordinary people in the pews—and for which there is no redress—are the failures which so powerfully convey the impression of a church without justice. Some familiar examples:

• schools closed without adequate consultation of parents;

• parishioners denied all voice in the life of their parish;

• parish communities without any serious attempt at Christian education or spiritual formation;

• communities subject consistently to woefully inadequate preaching, negligent and non-participatory liturgical celebrations;

• churches where no financial accounting is made to the people;

• parish staff persons terminated without evaluation or explanation;

• parish facilities denied to groups because the nature of their discussions is judged to be controversial;

• dioceses where there are no avenues for the expression of opinions or recommendations, no realistic participation in policy-making.

It is only fair to say that sometimes these abuses are alleged and not actual. Sometimes they are imagined or exaggerated or temporarily justified by circumstances. And sometimes almost nothing can be done about them because of the quality of available personnel or simple human frailty. But often such abuses are real and remedies are possible. Instead of responding to the complaints and vigorously seeking remedies, a bishop or pastor invokes the time-honored policy of stonewalling. The institution can always outlast the aggrieved individual. And the impression of callous unfairness grows.

Even when no solution to an abusive situation is evident, great good can be accomplished by a fair hearing. To have one's "day in court," to be taken seriously and treated with dignity, to be listened to and heard out—just that alone revives a sense of fairness and relieves powerlessness and alienation.

The abuses mentioned above are all rights failures. They are related to the rights claims of church members asserted in the 1983 Code. Rights which are declared but undefended are a mockery; when the claims cannot be vindicated, the rights are useless. Any society which fails to provide remedies for wrongs, reasonably adequate and available mechanisms for the redress of grievances, ways to insist on the basic claims which are constitutionally asserted, is not a just society. For those very reasons our church is perceived by many of its members, as well as by outside observers, to be an unjust church.

2. THE BILL OF RIGHTS IN THE 1983 CODE

The impressive list of rights and responsibilities of all the members of our church, placed dramatically at the very outset of the book on The People of God[3], possesses constitutional status. It has fundamental and constitutive import. It is far more than a declaration or manifesto, like the Declaration of the Rights of Man and of the Citizen (France, 1789) or the Universal Declaration of Human Rights (United Nations, 1948). These have had considerable exemplary, educational and idealistic impact. The Code's bill of rights should have those effects and more. It has greater weight than the exhortatory or statutory canons of the Code. The bill of rights is part of the bedrock upon which is based the rest of our canonical system.

The arguments to demonstrate the primacy of the canons on rights and responsibilities follow. But first one needs to recall that the canons of the Code have very different "juridic weights" (just as the physical elements possess varying atomic weights). Some canons are far more important than others. This is perfectly obvious even to the most casual observer. In spite of the fact that all of the canons look alike (same size type, same short paragraphs, all numbered sequentially from 1 to 1752), and that all were issued by the same authority, on the same day, in the same act of promulgation, they represent a variety of literary and theological forms (e.g., dogma, doctrine, discipline, exhortation, admonition, pious wish) and vastly different levels of value, seriousness and structural significance.[3] Compare canon 381 on the authority of a diocesan bishop with canon 571 which exhorts a chaplain to "maintain an appropriate close relationship with the pastor." In short, some rules of the Code set forth the very framework of Roman Catholic Church order while others state relatively trivial disciplinary preferences.

Now to the constitutional quality of the Bill of Rights. The arguments run along six lines:

a) The rights had their origin in the constitutional statement, *Lex Ecclesiae Fundamentalis* (The fundamental law of the Church);

b) They were uniquely mandated by the *Principia Quae Dirigant Recognitionem Codicis* (The principles which guide the revision of the Code);

c) *Sacrae Disciplinae Leges* (The Laws of the Sacred Discipline) asserts that the rights are a chief purpose of the Code;

d) They occur at the beginning of the book *De Populo Dei* (On the People of God) where membership and its characteristics are delineated;

e) Their content is of basic importance, that is, they are intrinsically fundamental claims;

f) John Paul II singled out the charter of rights for special attention just after the promulgation of the Code.

a) The celebrated *Lex Ecclesiae Fundamentalis* resembled a canonical space rocket.   It was launched under papal auspices, gained rapid momentum, rose high in the canonistic heavens, came under sharp attack, underwent repairs and mid-course corrections, and came crashing to earth to an unexplained demise, never to be heard from again.

Pope Paul VI himself suggested a canonical constitution to the Commission for the Revision of the Code even before the close of the Second Vatican Council.   He mentioned it specifically in his address of November 20, 1965, in which he propelled the revision process into action.   The Commission had a draft ready for discussion by the middle of 1966, and a revised version in the following year.   The 1967 Synod fathers urged the Commission on with the project.   After three more sessions on the subject the consultors presented a first formal draft to the Commission's cardinals by 1969.

Paul VI spoke of a "common and fundamental code containing the constitutive law (*ius constitutivum*) of the church" which was to underlie both the Eastern and Western (Latin) codes.[5]   It was clearly what we refer to as a constitution.

When the Commission made the first draft of the *Lex* public in the Spring of 1969 (*sub secreto,* but widely circulated), it contained a set of canons (numbers 10 to 24) which are substantially the same as those in the 1983 Code's Book II, canons 208 - 223.   Each one was identified with a source in the documents of the Vatican Council, mainly *Lumen Gentium,* by means of a footnote.   The official *Relatio* referred to this section as "The Fundamental Duties and Rights (*officia et iura*) of All of Christ's Faithful."   Subsequent drafts repeated this title.   They spoke of those canons defining and determining the primary duties and rights (*officia et iura primaria*) which pertain to all of the People of God, namely to all Christ's faithful.[6]

The Commission's communication to the Episcopal Synod of 1971 described the enumeration of rights of the faithful as fulfilling one of the chief purposes of the "fundamental code."[7]

The whole *Lex* project was put to death, without explanation, in 1981 after it had been approved by a specially convened international commission earlier in the year.   The canons on the rights and duties of members were transposed to the Code along with some elements from a set of rights which had been developed by the commission working on the text *On The People Of God.* In that process, the term *officia* (duties) was dropped in favor of *obligationes* (obligations), but the expression for rights, *iura*, remained the same.

The origins of the Code's bill of rights were not in a Constitutional Congress, but its history and development clearly reveal its truly constitutional character.

b) The Commission for Revision of the Code, as one of its first tasks, articulated a set of ten "principles to guide the revision" and submitted them to the 1967 Synod of Bishops. The Synod approved them by overwhelming votes.[8] Three of these ten directing principles dealt explicitly with the rights of members of the church:

i) The very first principle, which had to do with the juridic nature of the Code, states that "the principal and essential object of canon law is to define and safeguard the rights and obligations of each person toward others and toward society."[9]

ii) The sixth principle was specifically concerned with safeguarding the rights of persons. It began: "A very important problem is proposed to be solved in the future Code, namely how the rights of persons can be defined and safeguarded." It went on to say:

The use of power in the Church must not be arbitrary, because that is prohibited by the natural law, by divine positive law, and by ecclesiastical law. The rights of each one of Christ's faithful must be acknowledged and protected, both those which are contained in the natural and divine positive law and those derived from those laws because of the social condition which the faithful acquire and possess in the Church.[10]

In effect, the sixth principle explicitly called for a Bill of Rights in the new Code.

iii) The seventh principle had to do with established procedures for safeguarding subjective rights. In clarion tones it called for ready and realistic procedures for the actual vindication of personal rights:

The principle must be proclaimed in canon law that juridical protection applies equally to superiors and to

subjects so that any suspicion of arbitrariness in ecclesiastical administration will entirely disappear.

This end can only be achieved by avenues of recourse
wisely provided by the law which allow a person who
thinks his or her rights were violated at a lower level to
have them effectively restored at a higher level.[11]

The Commission went on to describe the need for better means of
administrative recourse, and specifically for various degrees and kinds
of administrative tribunals. Thus this principle set forth the need for
realistic and effective remedies for grievances in addition to the declaration and delineation of the rights themselves.

The prominent attention which the Commission and the Synod gave
to rights in advance of their formulation highlights the central importance they have in the new Code.

c) In his Apostolic Constitution *Sacrae Disciplinae Leges* which
promulgated the revised Code, John Paul II raised up the theme of the
rights of members of the church as a central accomplishment:

Among the elements which characterize the true and genuine
image of the Church we should emphasize especially the following: ". . . the doctrine according to which all the members of
the people of God, in the way suited to each one of them, participate in the threefold priestly, prophetic and kingly office of
Christ, to which doctrine is also linked that which concerns the
duties and rights of the faithful and particularly of the laity."[12]

And among the reasons why the Code is necessary for the church, the
pope stated:

Since the Church is organized as a social and visible structure,
it must also have norms: . . . in order that the mutual relations
of the faithful may be regulated according to justice based upon
charity, with the rights of individuals guaranteed and well-
defined.[13]

The special focus on the delineation and protection of rights in the
document of promulgation of the Code helps to support the charac-
terization of the rights section of Book II as constitutional.

d) In real estate location is everything. That is not true of the canons of the Code, but context does matter when it comes to understanding canons, as canon 17 states.[14] And the placement of the Bill of Rights in the Code does say something about its seriousness. It occurs at the very outset of the central and singularly important book of the Code, *De Populo Dei*. The canons on rights and obligations form part of the description of the very identity of the Christian faithful. Immediately after the Code defines who are the members of the church (canons 204 and 205), it sets forth the implications of that membership: the rights and obligations of those who are fully incorporated, fully in communion. Prior to the treatment of sacred ministers, before the rules on the hierarchical structure of the church, and well before the regulation of religious institutes, comes this threshold articulation of what it means to be a fully participating member of our church. In sum, the contextual situation of these canons shows them to be of foundational significance. To call them constitutional is not an exaggeration.

e) The rights stated in the Code are intrinsically of fundamental importance. They are concerned with matters basic to human dignity and to the meaning of church membership. Reflect on this listing of the rights and freedoms:

1. The fundamental equality of all Christians based on baptism, and equality and dignity in action; the right and freedom to cooperate in building up the Body of Christ (c. 208).

2. The right to evangelize the nations (c. 211).

3. The right to petition, that is, to make known to pastors one's needs (especially spiritual) and one's hopes (c. 212 #2).

4. The right to recommend: the right to advise pastors regarding the good of the church, and to participate in public opinion and informing the faithful (c. 212 #3).

5. The right to receive the Word of God and the sacraments from pastors (c. 213).

6. The right to participate in worship in accordance with legitimate norms of one's own rite (c. 214).

7. The right to one's proper spirituality (c. 214).

8. The right to association: the right to found and direct associations with charitable purposes and as an expression of Christian vocation (c. 215).

9. The right to assembly: the right to hold meetings for the same purpose as to associate (c. 215).

10. The right to promote the apostolate and to one's own proper initiative in apostolic work, based on the right to participate in the church's mission (c. 216).

11. The right to Christian education (c. 217).

12. Academic freedom: the right to research and to publication (c. 218).

13. Freedom from force in choosing one's station in life (c. 219).

14. The right to a good name and reputation (c. 220).

15. Privacy: the right to have others respect what is intimate to one's self (c. 220).

16. The right to vindicate one's rights in church court and to defend one's rights in church court (c. 221 #1) with equity and in accordance with law (c. 221 #2).

17. The right to be judged (c. 221 #2).

18. The right to legality regarding sanctions, that is, the right to expect the church to impose sanctions only in accordance with law (c. 221 #3).[15]

These rights and freedoms are not peripheral or inconsequential. They go to the heart of the reasons for belonging to a church. They are central to participation in a Christian community of faith and love. They are to life within the church what freedom of speech, freedom of religion, due process of law, suffrage and representation are to life as citizens. They are tantamount to what we are accustomed to refer to as constitutional rights.

f) Pope John Paul II called special attention to the Bill of Rights in his address to the Roman Rota just one month after the promulgation of the new Code:

The Church has always affirmed and protected the rights of the faithful. In the new code, indeed, she has promulgated them as a "fundamental charter" (*"carta fondamentale"*) (confer canons 208-223). She thus offers opportune judicial guarantees for protecting and safeguarding adequately the desired reciprocity between the rights and duties inscribed in the dignity of the person of the "faithful Christian."[16]

The mind of the legislator seems to be that this statement of the basic rights of the members of the church is of unique and fundamental importance.

The foregoing six lines of argumentation converge to a convincing conclusion: that the Code's Bill of Rights holds a genuinely constitutional status. It makes up an essential part of the fundamental order of our church, along with other foundational articulations in the Code.

What are the implications of constitutional status? Juridic priority. The rights of church members must be accorded a certain antecedence. They deserve and command juridical anteriority in relationship to other canonical dispositions. More concretely, when reflecting on a canonical action, before considering pastoral prerogatives or episcopal responsibilities or official duties, the first concern must be for the rights of the Christian faithful affected by the action. They have the primacy of constitutional claims.

Not only do these rights have to be taken seriously, they must also be safeguarded. They compel our attention and respect, but, more crucially, we must see that the rights receive the protection which befits constitutional guarantees. The practical means for the vindication of rights remains an urgent concern in our church. More about that below.

3. OUR TRADITION ON RIGHTS

Much in the Roman Catholic tradition recommends taking rights seriously. Popular impressions to the contrary notwithstanding, the personal claims of members of our church have frequently been proclaimed, honored and vindicated both in theory and in practice. The teaching and the discipline of our church strongly support rights claims. For the present purpose three examples will serve to illuminate this tradition: a) two passages from the New Testament writings, b) a glance at the medieval canonists, and c) the modern social teaching on human rights.

a) In the young community of Christians at Corinth it happened that disputes between members were taken into the secular courts of the city for resolution. When the Apostle Paul learned of this, he took strong exception:

> How can anyone with a case against another dare bring it for judgment to the wicked and not to God's holy people? . . . Can it be that there is no one among you wise enough to settle a case between one member of the church and another? Must brother drag brother into court and before unbelievers at that? [17]

"It is a brazen act, Paul declares, for one Christian to enter a lawsuit against another Christian before a pagan court."[18] It bespeaks an indifference to the requirements of unity and communion in Christian society. Paul wants Christians to resolve their differences among themselves. He might prefer that they simply turn the other cheek, forgive, and avoid seeking any redress at all, but if the dispute must be settled, it should be done within the community of believers.

Paul has in mind that people in the church should choose mediators or judges acceptable to both disputing parties, and he wants to assure that the judges would be those who had standing in the church on the basis of proper spiritual qualification. "The Christian mediator should have in view the reconciliation of the parties that they might get rightly related to the forgiving and loving God by forgiving one another."[19]

In Paul's view such incidents as taking disputes between Christians to the pagan law courts bring the witness and communion of the church into disrepute among pagans, and harm the spirit of communion within the church. If the unity, peace and communion within the church cannot be preserved in a spirit of Christian love and forgiveness, how can the church fulfill its mission among the nations of the world?[20]

Matthew's gospel also refers to the situation of injuries or grievances occurring within the community of faith. A procedure for the resolution of such problems, derived from Jewish rules of evidence, is outlined:

> If your neighbor should commit some wrong against you, go and point out the fault, but keep it between the two of you. If he or she listens to you, you have won your neighbor over. If your neighbor does not listen, summon another, so that every case may stand on the word of two or three witnesses. If he or

she ignores them, refer it to the church. If he or she ignores even the church, then treat him or her as you would a Gentile or a tax collector.[21]

The saying concerns personal offenses and the willingness for or refusal of reconciliation within the local community.[22] The witnesses are to attest the neighbor's readiness to forgive and be reconciled, not to give evidence of the injury or wrong. The process is a part of the community's own discipline, and it indicates the sensitivity to the resolution of disputes which was present in the earliest Christian churches.[23]

To read a "theory of rights" into these texts about dispute resolution in two New Testament churches would probably be unwarranted. But the references are to personal harm or perceived wrongs, and the careful attention paid to the manner of their settlement within the community shows that matters involving what we now call "rights" were taken quite seriously.

b) "The twelfth and thirteenth centuries were an age not only of increasing awareness of rights but of the rise of the legal science that provided the means of asserting rights in court."[24] Canonists participated in and contributed to this development in a major way.[25]

Harold Berman, in *Law and Revolution: The Formation of the Western Legal Tradition*,[26] asserts that "the first modern Western legal system was the canon law of the Roman Catholic Church."[27] He describes at length the growth of the canonical system, which he relates to the "Papal Revolution" (i.e., the Gregorian Reform, 1050-1122 A.D.), and the considerable impact which its innovations, procedures and principles made on the further shaping of western law.[28]

The canonical system had long historical and theological roots, but its rules arose from the life of the people:

Out of the system of ecclesiastical constitutional law there gradually developed relatively coherent bodies of substantive rules . . . . There also developed rules of judicial procedure. These bodies of law were not conceptualized in the same way that autonomous branches of law came to be conceptualized in later centuries: the canonists of the twelfth and thirteenth centuries did not attempt to organize each branch of law—property, contract, crime, and so forth—as a self-contained set of rules stemming logically from various principles and doctrines . . . .

The canon law was less abstract, less "logical." Its categories had grown out of the jurisdiction of the ecclesiastical courts and out of the legal problems confronting those courts rather than out of the speculative reasoning of academic jurists. . . . the canon law tended to be systematized more on the basis of procedure than of substantive rules.[29]

Berman mentions three interesting examples of this process of evolving procedural law. One was the process of "prorogation" by which the church offered the benefit of its jurisdiction to all who wished to choose it. Parties to any civil dispute could, by agreement, submit their dispute to an ecclesiastical court or to ecclesiastical arbitration. Parties to civil contracts often wrote in clauses providing in advance for such submissions.

In addition, according to canon law any person could bring suit in an ecclesiastical court, or remove a case from a secular court to an ecclesiastical court, even against the will of the other party, on the ground of "default of secular justice." Thus the church ultimately offered its jurisdiction and its law to anyone for any type of case, but only under exceptional circumstances, that is, when justice itself, in the most elementary sense, was at stake.[30]

One of the advances which canon law provided beyond the earlier Roman procedures and Germanic customs was a simplified process:

The canonists also invented the concept of a dual system of procedure, one solemn and formal, the other simple and equitable. The simple procedure was available for certain types of civil cases, including those involving poor or oppressed persons and those for which an ordinary legal remedy was not available. It dispensed with legal counsel as well as with written pleadings and written interrogatories.[31]

Eventually the canonists did the speculative reasoning which led to legal theories. Henry of Susa, better known as Cardinal Hostiensis, was one of the most highly respected canonists of the "golden age of canon law." He was a "decretalist" (i.e., a commentator on the Decretals of Pope Gregory IX, 1234), active from about 1230 to 1271. When Hostiensis wrote on the purpose of law he focused on the need for declaring rights and protecting them with fair procedures. He quoted Gregory's own intentions in promulgating his collection of decretals:

> Laws are given so that harmful passions might be restrained under the rule of law, so that humankind might be trained to live decently, that we might not harm one another, and that each one might be given his or her due.[32]

Hostiensis added that laws are to protect the innocent from the dishonest, to show compassion for the oppressed, to see to it that justice is done in the courts (and excessive costs and delays avoided therein), to avoid discord and to remedy frauds.[33]

Clarence Gallagher, in his study of the legal views of Hostiensis in his most influential work, the *Summa Aurea*, points out the great canonist's concern for the "delineation of rights and duties and legal protection through due process."[34] Hostiensis frequently repeated the widely accepted maxim that "it does little good to have rights in society unless there is someone to make them real."[35]

The canonical collections and commentaries of the middle ages were filled with clarifications of rights and duties and the procedures to pursue them. Nearly all of the rules were for the hierarchy, the clergy and religious, the chapters and synods, the officials and courts. There was no "Bill of Rights" for the members of the church. But the medieval canonists had a keen concern for justice, developed a sense of individual and collective rights, and made great strides toward due process.

c) Our church's modern social teaching provides a sound basis for the right claims in the revised Code. David Hollenbach's study, *Claims in Conflict: Retrieving and Renewing the Catholic Human Rights Tradition*,[36] exposes this facet of our doctrine and traces its development over the past one hundred years. This teaching possesses a soundness, consistency and elegance which commands respect, but it also stands as a challenge to the inner life of the church.

The centerpiece and foundational principle of the modern Catholic tradition on human rights is the dignity of the human person. This primary truth runs through the entire teaching on rights.

> The thread that ties all these documents together is their common concern for the protection of the dignity of the human person. In a speech delivered in May, 1961, John XXIII stated that

the entire modern tradition "is always dominated by one basic theme—an unshakable affirmation and vigorous defense of the dignity and rights of the human person." In John XXIII's view, human dignity is the concrete normative value which the entire tradition has attempted to defend. Respect for the dignity and worth of the person is the foundation of all the specific human rights and more general social ethical frameworks adopted by the encyclicals and other Church teachings.[37]

This central and fundamental truth has not been simply repeated; it has been nuanced and developed through the decades. Pope Leo XIII's encyclicals (chiefly *Rerum Novarum*, 1891) laid the groundwork for the modern Catholic theory of human rights. Human dignity is the foundation of his theory of human rights. In both the political and economic spheres he interpreted the demands of human dignity with the help of an analysis of the impact of social, economic and political institutions on human persons.[38]

Pius XI, facing different world problems forty years later (*Quadragesimo Anno*, 1931), added a new dimension to our human rights heritage. He held that the notion of social justice as a regulative principle for societal institutions is based on the conviction that human dignity is a social rather than a purely private affair. Human dignity makes a genuine moral demand upon the organizational patterns by which public life is structured. Pius XI's writings represented a major development in the tradition's recognition of the social conditions and limits which enter into the specification of the meaning of human dignity and human rights.[39]

During and after the agony of the Second World War Pius XII reflected on human rights and government's role in maintaining them. The order which he saw as the concrete realization of social morality is a juridical or constitutional order of rights. The realization of such an order is a duty incumbent on all persons, and this duty is to be carried out in a partial but very important way through constitutional government. The role of government is the promotion of the common good— that form of society in which responsible citizens act in a way which leads to mutual respect for rights and dignity. The common good, since it is founded on mutual dignity, is not in opposition to human rights, but rather their guarantee. This role of the common good and the role of government in protecting it shows that, for Pius XII as well as for the entire tradition, human rights cannot be understood apart from social interdependence, nor can social well-being be understood apart from personal rights. This approach introduced a strong emphasis on the developmental and dynamic character of rights.[40]

Pope John XXIII further nuanced the Catholic teaching on rights by insisting on the interdependence of societal factors in their support for rights and by specifying the rights more explicitly and completely than ever before. The single basic norm of respect for human dignity led him to understand both civil-political rights and social-economic rights within a single integrated theoretical framework. *Pacem in Terris* (1963) maintained that the protection and coordination of human rights are increasingly a task which calls for organized action within society as a whole. The list of rights articulated in *Pacem in Terris* represents a systematic recapitulation of the rights claims made by the tradition since Leo XIII.[41]

The Second Vatican Council plunged the rights discussion into the reality of history by acknowledging that the demands of human dignity are historically conditioned. *Gaudium et spes* (1965) taught that if persons in society possess a transcendental worth, then the structures of social organization are confronted with claims to serve and protect this personal dignity. The precise content of these claims, however, is historically conditioned. Thus it is impossible to specify the conditions of human dignity *a priori*. Any justification of particular claims that would grant them the status of rights involves a measure of historical judgment.[42]

Pope Paul VI's chief statements on human rights were contained in *Populorum Progressio* (1967) and *Octagesima Adveniens* (1971). In them he stressed the concept of "integral development," raised human material needs to a new level of importance, and emphasized that rights can be realized only in social collaboration. The human personality is multifaceted. The protection of human dignity, therefore, requires respect for the multiple social, economic, intellectual, interpersonal and religious conditions of personal development. Material well-being is not simply an instrumental value, simply a means to a dignified life. Rather it is integral to the standard of all moral value, human dignity. Human rights, therefore, are expressions of the more fundamental moral experience of human solidarity. Whether these rights be negative immunities or positive entitlement they presuppose that persons recognize that they are bound together in a moral community of mutual inter-dependence. [43]

The statement, *Justice in the World*, of the 1971 Synod of Bishops added the fundamental and complex notions of the right of participation and the right of development. Marginalization or lack of participation has become a primary criterion for judging if human dignity is being violated. Lack of adequate nourishment, housing, education and political self-determination are seen as a consequence of this lack of participation. The relational quality of human dignity was spelled out by the Synod in terms of a fundamental right to participation which integrates all the other rights with each other and provides their operational foundation. The right to development affirmed by the Synod is the first specification of the demands of dignity in the present historical situation. Respect for persons demands active participation in the process of social change and development. The right to development is a comparative right; its content can only be discovered by regarding the individual person within his or her own social context and in relation to other persons. The rights to participation and development have become conditions for the realization of all other rights. [44]

For our present purpose the 1971 Synod document is of special significance, for it explicitly insists that rights be fully respected in the internal structures and procedures of the church. In this context it affirms the right to a just wage, the right to participation, the rights of women, the rights to freedom of expression and thought, and the right to due process of law. [45] The Synod urged us to take justice claims seriously, and to work for the rights of persons *within the church* as well as in the civil order. Its words are both familiar and challenging to us.

> While the Church is bound to give witness to justice, she recognizes that anyone who ventures to speak to people about justice must first be just in their eyes. Hence we must undertake an examination of the modes of acting and of the possessions and life style found within the Church herself.

> Within the Church rights must be preserved. [46]

The constitutional rights declared in the 1983 Code find firm footing in modern Catholic social teaching. In fact, the 1971 Synod statement brings these theories home and insists that they are to be applied *within* the community of faith.

The foregoing samplings from our tradition—the New Testament churches, the medieval canonists, modern social teaching—demonstrate that human rights claims and their procedural protections are quite in keeping with that tradition. "Rights talk" is familiar language for Catholics; what is needed is to move from conversation to effective action in the life of the church.

4. A CONTEMPORARY DISCUSSION OF RIGHTS

In the last fifteen years a remarkable literature has sprung up in the area of political theory.[47] These highly intelligent and plausible speculations of philosophers, political scientists and students of government have resulted in both a rich literature and a lively discussion, one which spills over from the ivory towers of academia to more practical levels of political debate. The ultimate concern of most of this writing is the area of distributive justice: What does a society owe its members? How are the resources to be equitably distributed? How are the disadvantaged to be treated: the poor, the ill, the old, the young, the handicapped? These radical and politically sensitive issues are the final preoccupations of the debate, but along the way the participants are forced to reflect upon and define basic concepts like liberties, claims and rights.

John Rawls is probably the most celebrated of these contemporary theorists. His book, *A Theory of Justice,* published in 1971, seems to have sparked the debate. As Robert Nozick, another major voice in the discussion, wrote in 1974, "Political philosophers now must either work within Rawls' theory or explain why not."[48] But many others have contributed to the scholarly dialogue: some social contract theorists, some natural law proponents, some utilitarians. It is a dense and intriguing discourse.

The whole enterprise can be envisioned as an attempt to bridge the chasm between liberal democratic theories which prize civil and political rights, and Marxist theories which give primary emphasis to social and economic rights. This sharp conflict of political theories, which divides the socialist/communist regimes from the capitalist democracies of the world, was consciously papered over by the 1948 United Nations Declaration of Human Rights. These contemporary theorists are trying to build a bridge between these two worlds, or, rather, to construct a middle ground so that a truly just society can emerge.

Canonists should be aware of this learned, largely secular discussion; we should take part in it, and we certainly can learn from it as we ponder the issues related to rights in our church. By way of a single example, can we adopt the view of John Rawls in our approach to canonical rights?

> Justice is the first virtue of social institutions, as truth is of systems of thought. A theory, however elegant and economical, must be rejected or revised if it is untrue; likewise laws and institutions, no matter how efficient and well-arranged, must be reformed or abolished if they are unjust. Each person possesses an inviolability founded on justice that even the welfare of society as a whole cannot override.[49]

Rawls declares that the first principle of that justice which is at the basis of any society is "equality in the assignment of basic rights and duties,"[50] and that "each person is to have an equal right to the most extensive basic liberty compatible with a similar liberty for others."[51]

5. PRACTICAL PROPOSALS

Both Francis Morrisey and Ladislas Orsy, writing recently on the subject of rights in the church, stressed the need for innovations at the practical level in order to make the rights real.

> Indeed, rights are of little avail if they cannot be implemented or vindicated when necessary. Probably here more than anywhere else in the new code will we have to change our way of thinking. It is not simply a question of pouring new wine into old skins: present mechanisms in many instances are simply unable to cope with this new and fascinating dimension of Church law. Some form of recourse will have to become available to ensure that rights are respected.[52]

Orsy wrote of the need to go beyond theology and theory about rights and work toward "practical legal means to redress any violation speedily," to work "toward setting up an efficient judicial machinery to uphold fundamental rights and to enforce fundamental duties. The aim is concrete action. The field of inquiry is the practical demands of justice."[53]

The following two suggestions attempt to meet the need to take rights seriously by providing realistic means for their vindication.

a) Adapt our existing diocesan tribunals to adjudicate a variety of disputes besides those involving the nullity of the bond of marriage.

Canon 221 states that "the Christian faithful can legitimately vindicate and defend the rights which they enjoy in the Church before a competent ecclesiastical court in accord with the norm of law." The canon could not be clearer. The church's courts are to be open to the rights claims of church members. Believers are to receive justice in the tribunals of their church. But in fact our courts are not accessible to them in instances of the violation of their rights. The courts only hear marriage cases, and that is all they are prepared to hear.

Since the Code gives a mandate to make the courts accessible, we should not shrink back from or delay doing so. And to broaden the scope of their activity, to accept and decide other kinds of disputes may not be as awesome a prospect as is often imagined.[54] A brief comment on three elements of our judicial process may be in order here: on personnel, on procedures, and on a learning process.

Each community recognizes within it certain of its members who are almost universally respected; they seem to embody a Christian wisdom, maturity, objectivity and common sense. Such persons are trusted implicitly, and their opinions are valued. They could function effectively as judges without their having to be experts in canon law or in the areas of human conflict. Their decisions in the forum of the tribunal would be honored. A few in each diocese would suffice; cases should not be frequent.

The Code offers a speedier and simpler process than the ordinary one for contentious cases. The oral contentious process (canons 1656 to 1670; derived from the early fourteenth century) is designed to provide a fair hearing and a prompt decision with a minimum of preparation, time lapse or record keeping. It might serve as an effective procedure for resolving many disputes quickly and "in accord with the norm of the law."

A learning process will be required, because few persons have experienced the use of church courts for a diversity of cases. Sharing cases, procedures and results will be vital; tribunals will learn from one another just as they have done with marriage cases.

The same pastoral sensitivity, dedication and ingenuity which has so vastly improved tribunal performance in reconciling those who have experienced the tragedy of divorce could become a powerful force in shaping a more just church.

b) Create alternative means of conflict resolution and grievance redress.

The revised Code provides ample warrant for setting up and utilizing other kinds of procedures for the settlement of rights claims. "With due regard for justice, all the Christian faithful, especially bishops, are to strive earnestly to avoid lawsuits among the people of God as much as possible, and to resolve them peacefully as soon as possible" (canon 1446, #1). The second paragraph of the same canon urges the judge "to encourage and assist the parties to collaborate in working out an equitable solution to the controversy . . . even employing the services of reputable persons for mediation." The third paragraph instructs the judge to ascertain whether the litigation can "be resolved through a negotiated settlement or through arbitration."

Under the title, "Methods of Avoiding a Trial," the Code recommends a process of settlement or reconciliation by means of arbitration (canons 1713 to 1716). And again, when the Code treats of administrative recourse, conciliation or arbitration are given as very desirable means to resolve contentious differences (canon 1733, #1). The second paragraph of the same canon provides for the establishment of permanent offices or councils in each diocese for the purpose of working out equitable solutions to administrative grievances.

These canons recall the due process procedures elaborated by the Canon Law Society of America[55] and approved for diocesan use by the National Conference of Catholic Bishops in 1969.[56] These processes have been successfully employed in several dioceses in the intervening years;[57] the very existence of grievance procedures has been perceived as beneficial in many places. The lack of any effective sharing of the experiences of these processes is lamentable; it limits the possibilities of learning, imitation and improvement.

Other resources also are available in our society; the services of the American Arbitration Association are among them.[58] We must search for simple and expeditious procedures which safeguard fairness and give adequate hearing but avoid the pitfalls of cumbersomeness, expensive transcription, excessive delays and adversarial postures.

These two "suggestions" are not really voluntary options; they are integral parts of the current discipline of our church. They are canonical requirements. More importantly, they are urgently needed for the protection of the rights of the Christian faithful.

Will we try to make our church more just for all its people? We have a new canonical "Bill of Rights." It is part of the church's constitutional structure. And it resonates with the church's authentic tradition. Will we try to make the rights real for our people? We must improvise new procedures and put old ones to new purposes. We can learn from our own past, from secular parallels, from other churches.

Pope John Paul II spoke to the Dutch church recently about liberty and law: "Christ established his church as a well-ordered and free people," he said.[59] "Christ called us to true freedom. He alone can make us truly free. That is why the church gives so much care throughout the world to defending and furthering authentic human liberty."[60] What our church attempts throughout the world we must assure at home: respect for the rights of Christ's faithful, and the means to make those rights real. Only then will we actually be a free and well-ordered people.[61]

Notes

1. Reprinted, with permission, from "The Jurist," Vol. 45, No. 1, 1985.

2. Recent writings on rights in the Church include:

J. Beyer, "De statuto iuridico Christifidelium iuxta nota Synodi Episcoporum in novo Codice Iuris condendo," PERIODICA 57 (1968), pp. 550-581.

J. Coriden, ed., THE CASE FOR FREEDOM: HUMAN RIGHTS IN THE CHURCH, Washington: Corpus, 1969.

J. Kinney, "Rights and Duties of the Faithful in the Schema 'People of God': An Encouragement to Exercise Them," CLSA PROCEEDINGS (1980), pp. 107-114.

R. Schwarz, "Circa Naturam Iuris Subjectivi," PERIODICA 69 (1980), pp. 191-200.

E. Corecco et al., eds., LES DROITS FONDAMENTAUX DU CHRETIEN DANS L'ÉGLISE ET DANS LA SOCIÉTÉ. Actes du IVe Congrès International de Droit Canonique, Fribourg: Ed. Universitaires Fribourg, 1981.

J. Provost, "Ecclesial Rights," CLSA PROCEEDINGS (1982), pp. 41-62.

R. Bertolino, LA TUTELA DEI DIRITTI NELLA CHIESA: DAL VEC-CHIO AL NUOVO CODICE DI DIRITTO CANONICO, Torino: Giappichelli, 1983.

J. Tinako, "The Fundamental Rights and Obligations of the Faithful," PHILIP-PINIANA SACRA, (1983), pp. 392-416.
P. Valdrini, INJUSTICES ET PROTECTION DES DROITS DANS L'ÉGLISE, Strasbourg: Cerdic, 1983.

3. Canons 208 through 223.

4. L. Orsy, "The Interpreter and His Art," JURIST 40 (1980), pp. 33-40.

5. AAS, 57 (1965), p. 988.

6. Pont. Comm. Cod. Iur, Can. Recog., SCHEMA LEGIS ECCLESIAE FUNDA-MENTALIS CUM RELATIONE, Rome: Typ. Poly. Vat., 1969, p. 79.

7. Idem, COMMUNICATIO DE SCHEMATE "LEGIS ECCLESIAE FUNDA-MENTALIS."

8. COMMUNICATIONES 1 (1969), pp. 77-100. PATRIBUS SYNODI EPISCO-PORUM HABENDA, Typ. Poly. Vat., 1971, p. 8.

9. Ibid., p. 79.

10. Ibid., p. 82.

11. Ibid., p. 83.

12. CODE OF CANON LAW, LATIN-ENGLISH EDITION, Washington: CLSA, 1983, p. xv.

13. Ibid.

14. "Ecclesiastical laws are to be understood in accord with the proper meaning of the words considered in their text and context."

15. B. Griffin, "A Bill of Rights and Freedoms," CODE, COMMUNITY, MINIS-TRY, J. Provost, ed., Washington: CLSA, 1983, pp. 28-29.

16. AAS 75 (1983) 556; ORIGINS 12 (1983), p. 631.

17. I Cor. 6, 1-6.

18. W. F. Orr & J. A. Walther, I CORINTHIANS. The Anchor Bible, vol.32, New York: Doubleday, 1976, p. 195.

19. Ibid., p. 197.

20. THE INTERPRETER'S BIBLE, vol. X, New York: Abingdon Press, 1953, p. 70.

21. Matt. 18:15-17, adapted.

22. W. F. Albright & C. A. Mann, MATTHEW. The Anchor Bible, vol. 26, New York: Doublday, 1971, p. 220.

23. "A continuous thread runs through most of Matthew's material—a thread of concern for the right ordering of the community founded by Jesus." Ibid., pp. LXXXII-LXXXIII. Confer also on this passage, W. Thompson, MATTHEW'S ADVICE TO A DIVIDED COMMUNITY: Mt. 17, 22—18, 35, Rome: Biblical Institute Press, 1970, pp. 175-202.

24. G. Post, STUDIES IN MEDIEVAL LEGAL THOUGHT: PUBLIC LAW AND THE STATE, 1100-1322. Princeton: Princeton Univ. Press, 1964, p. 82.

25. For example, confer: B. Tierney, RELIGION, LAW AND THE GROWTH OF CONSTITUTIONAL THOUGHT, Cambridge: Cambridge Univ. Press, 1982, p. 37; C. Morris, THE DISCOVERY OF THE INDIVIDUAL, 1050-1200, New York: Harper & Row, 1972, p. 3, 6; W. Ullmann, THE INDIVIDUAL AND SOCIETY IN THE MIDDLE AGES, Baltimore: Johns Hopkins Press, 1966, pp. 129ss; R. Tuck, NATURAL RIGHTS THEORIES: THEIR ORIGIN AND DEVELOPMENT, Cambridge: Cambridge Univ. Press, 1979, p. 15.

26. Harold Berman, LAW AND REVOLUTION: THE FORMATION OF THE WESTERN LEGAL TRADITION, Cambridge: Harvard Univ. Press, 1983.

27. Ibid., p. 44.

28. Ibid., pp. 85-254.

29. Ibid., pp. 225-226.

30. Ibid., p. 223.

31. Ibid, pp. 250-251.

32. "Ideoque lex proditur ut appetitus noxius sub juris regula limitetur, per quam genus humanum ut honeste vivat, alterum non laedat, ius suum unicuique tribuat, informatur." Quoted in C. Gallagher, CANON LAW AND THE CHRISTIAN COMMUNITY: THE ROLE OF LAW IN THE CHURCH ACCORDING TO THE SUMMA AUREA OF CARDINAL HOSTIENSIS, Rome: Gregorian Univ. Press, 1978, p. 82.

33. Ibid., p. 82-84.

34. Ibid., pp. 125ff.

35. "Parum prodest iura habere in civitate nisi sit qui iura reddat." Ibid., p. 162.

36. D. Hollenbach, CLAIMS IN CONFLICT: RETRIEVING AND RENEWING THE CATHOLIC HUMAN RIGHTS TRADITION, New York: Paulist Press, 1979.

37. Ibid., p. 42.

38. Ibid., p. 49.

39. Ibid., pp. 55-56.

40. Ibid., pp. 60-61.

41. Ibid., pp. 66-67.

42. Ibid., p. 70.

43. Ibid., pp. 79-81.

44. Ibid., pp. 86-87.

45. Ibid., p. 89.

46. JUSTICE IN THE WORLD, nos. 40-41. For more on the theological basis for human rights, confer Hollenbach, CLAIMS IN CONFLICT, pp. 107-137; A. Hennelly & J. Langan, HUMAN RIGHTS IN THE AMERICAS: THE STRUGGLE FOR CONSENSUS, Washington: Georgetown Univ. Press, 1982; A. Miller, A CHRISTIAN DECLARATION ON HUMAN RIGHTS: THEOLOGICAL STUDIES OF THE WORLD ALLIANCE OF REFORMED CHURCHES, Grand Rapids: Eerdmans, 1977.

47. Some of the major monographs:

J. Feinberg, DOING AND DESERVING, Princeton: Princeton Univ. Press, 1970;

idem, RIGHTS, JUSTICE, AND THE BOUNDS OF LIBERTY, Princeton Univ. Press, 1980;

J. Rawls, A THEORY OF JUSTICE, Cambridge: Harvard Univ. Press, 1971;

R. Nozick, ANARCHY, STATE, AND UTOPIA, New York: Basic Books, 1974.

R. Flathman, THE PRACTICE OF RIGHTS, Cambridge: Cambridge Univ. Press, 1976;

D. Miller, SOCIAL JUSTICE, Oxford: Clarendon Press, 1976;

R. Dworkin, TAKING RIGHTS SERIOUSLY, Cambridge: Harvard Univ. Press, 1978;

idem, HUMAN RIGHTS: ESSAYS ON JUSTIFICATION AND APPLICATION, Chicago: Univ. of Chicago Press, 1982;

R. Tuck, NATURAL RIGHTS THEORIES: THEIR ORIGIN AND DEVELOPMENT, Cambridge: Cambridge Univ. Press, 1979;

W. Gallston, JUSTICE AND THE HUMAN GOOD, Chicago: Univ. of Chicago Press, 1980;

J. Finnis, NATURAL LAW AND NATURAL RIGHTS, Oxford: Clarendon Press, 1980;

J. R. Lucas, ON JUSTICE, Oxford: Clarendon Press, 1980;

J. Sterba, THE DEMANDS OF JUSTICE, Notre Dame: Univ. of Notre Dame Press, 1980;

T. Benditt, RIGHTS, Totowa, NJ: Rowman & Littlefield, 1982.

48. Nozick, ANARCHY, p. 183.

49. Rawls, A THEORY, p. 3.

50. Ibid., p. 14.

51. Ibid., p. 60.

52. F. Morrisey, "The Laity in the New Code of Canon Law," STUDIA CANONICA 17 (1983), p. 139.

53. L. Orsy, "Fundamental Rights in the Church: Personal Report on the Convention of the International Association of the Study of Canon Law," JURIST 41 (1981), pp. 181, 184.

54. For example, James Biechler of La Salle University., Philadelphia, has had the local tribunal look into intra-Church collective-bargaining agreements.

55. C/O Catholic University of America, Washington D.C. 20064. (202) 269-3491.

56. ON DUE PROCESS, Washington: NCCB, 1971.

57. T. Molloy, "The Theological Foundation of Ecclesiastical Due Process," CLSA PROCEEDINGS 41 (1979), pp. 60-67.

58. A.A.A. 140 W. 51 St., N.Y. N.Y. 10020. (212) 484-4000 —branches in many major cities.

59. s, Hertogenbosch, May 11, 1985; ORIGINS 15/2 (May 20, 1985), p. 19.

60. Ibid., p. 20.

61. The following essays on ARCC's Charter of Rights are an attempt to elaborate on what is already in the Code about rights. It is hoped that the essays will contribute to the discussion about rights in the Church and help to make it a luminous example of what a just society should be.

1. Following Conscience

Anthony R. Kosnik

All Catholics have the right to follow their informed consciences in all matters (C. 748.1).

The single most compelling statement regarding the freedom of Catholics to follow their informed consciences is found in Vatican II's Pastoral Constitution on the Church in the Modern World:

> Man has in his heart a law written by God. To obey it is the very dignity of man; according to it he will be judged. Conscience is the most secret core and sanctuary of man. There he is alone with God, whose voice echoes in his depths. In a wonderful manner conscience reveals that law which is fulfilled by love of God and neighbor. In fidelity to conscience, Christians are joined with the rest of men in search for truth, and for the genuine solution to the numerous problems which arise in the life of individuals and from social relationships (*Gaudium et Spes*, 16).

The importance of this right, especially for our times, is further emphasized in the opening lines of the Declaration on Religious Freedom:

> A sense of the dignity of the human person has been impressing itself more and more deeply on the consciousness of contem-

---

Anthony R. Kosnik is a priest of the Archdiocese of Detroit and directs the Pastoral Ministry Program at Marygrove College, Marygrove, MI.

porary man. And the demand is increasingly made that men should act on their own judgement, enjoying and making use of a responsible freedom, not driven by coercion but motivated by a sense of duty, *(Dignitatis Humanae, 1).*

As both documents attest, this right of freedom of conscience is not a recent discovery or declaration of the Church. The right itself is rooted in the very nature and dignity of what it means to be human and pre-exists the Church. The Church does not grant this right but simply acknowledges it. It is the God-given source of true human dignity and the only valid foundation for real community and for a genuine solution to the problems of the world. In this sense, freedom of conscience is not merely a right; it is also a sacred and serious responsibility.

Catholic tradition has always acknowledged this right in theory, even though it may not always have honored it in practice. As early as the third century, Lactantius reacted to the Roman law enforcing religious sacrifice declaring: "Unless the act is done freely and from the heart it is an accursed abomination," ("Divinarum Institutionum," V. 19, in Migne *Patrologia Latina, VI*, 20 cols. 614-16).

In the Middle Ages Thomas Aquinas similarly taught that, "Anyone upon whom the ecclesiastical authorities, in ignorance of the true facts, impose a demand against his clear conscience should perish in excommunication rather than violate his conscience." (IV Sent. dist. 38 art. 4 expos. text).

Through the centuries theological manuals have insisted that a "certain" i.e., formed conscience must be followed even if it is in error. To refuse to follow a certain conscience is clearly sin. To refuse to inform one's conscience through culpable neglect or ignorance is, of course, inexcusable.

In most recent times (1963) John XXIII re-affirmed the absolute inviolability of the right to freedom of conscience regarding internal acts in *Pacem in Terris*:

Since by nature all men are equal in human dignity, it follows that no one may be coerced to perform interior acts. That is in the power of God alone, who sees and judges the hidden designs of men's hearts *(Pacem in Terris, 48)*.

The new Revised Code of Canon Law gives canonical sanction to this right in Canon 748:

1. All persons are bound to seek the truth in matters concerning God and God's Church; by divine law they also are obliged and have the right to embrace and to observe that truth which they have recognized.

2. Persons cannot ever be forced by anyone to embrace the Catholic faith against their conscience.

In circumstances where the exercise of this right will infringe upon the rights of others or endanger the common good, legitimate authority may rightfully restrain the external exercise of that freedom. But the far greater responsibility of authority is to create the conditions and atmosphere where all members of society can exercise their right freely and responsibly.

Discussion Questions

1. What are the strongest arguments against the right to freedom of conscience and how would you respond to them?

2. In the light of your personal experience, what factors most effectively contributed to the development of your freedom of conscience and what factors most inhibited this development?

3. What options or actions should an individual take in a society or community that militates against the freedom of conscience?

Bibliography

1. William C. Bier, S. J., ed., CONSCIENCE: ITS FREEDOM AND LIMITATIONS. New York: Fordham University Press, 1971.

2. D'Arcy, Eric. CONSCIENCE AND ITS RIGHT TO FREEDOM. New York: Sheed & Ward, 1961.

3. C. Ellis Nelson, ed., CONSCIENCE: THEOLOGICAL AND PSYCHOLOGICAL PERSPECTIVES. New York: Newman Press, 1973.

2. Private and Public Morality

Ronald Modras

Officers of the Church have the right to teach on matters both of private and public morality only after wide consultation prior to the formulation of their teaching (C. 212, C. 747, C. 749, C. 752, C. 774.1).

The rights of bishops and the pope are interrelated here with those of the rest of the Church. Office-holders in the Church have the right to teach not only the gospel but also the moral principles that follow from it (C. 747). This right implies the obligation on the part of Catholics to give "religious respect" to the teachings of the pope and bishops, even when they do not teach infallibly (LG[1] 25; C. 752). Religious respect here does not mean blind obedience or the same kind of assent we give to God's revelation, since non-infallible teaching may be erroneous. But it does call for serious consideration of the teaching, respect for the bishops' teaching office, and, when one is in doubt, a presumption of truth and good judgment on the part of the bishops (HL[2] 18).

The right of the bishops to teach is not unilateral or absolute, however. Both Vatican Council II and the Revised Code of Canon Law acknowledge the right of Catholics to seek the truth (C. 748) and to follow

---

Ronald Modras is a priest of the Archdiocese of Detroit and is Associate Professor of Theological Studies at St. Louis University.

their conscience (DH[3] 1). Here the claim is raised to the right of the rest of the Church to be consulted before the bishops formulate their teaching. The basis for this claim is the teaching of the Council that the whole people of God and not just the clergy share in the prophetic office and teaching ministry of Christ. "A supernatural sense of the faith... characterizes the People as a whole" (LG[1] 2).

Consultation resulting in collaboration by pastors and people in discerning truth and the will of God has a long history in the Church. The Acts of the Apostles relates how time and again not only the apostles but all the church participated in decision-making (Acts 6:3,9; 8:4; 13:1-3; 15:22). The reason for this was the conviction that the spirit of God has been poured out not only upon the leaders but upon all believers, young and old alike (Acts 2:16-18). The concept of a hierarchy of leaders separated from laity did not exist in the New Testament church. All members had gifts of the Spirit and the responsibility to use them on behalf of the community (1 Cor. 12:4-31).

Subsequent tradition reveals that the New Testament model of consultation continued in the early church. "A bishop must not be imposed on people against their will," St. (Pope) Celestine I declared. Pope Leo the Great was of the same mind: "He who is to be the overseer of all must be chosen by all." St. Cyprian ministered as the bishop of Carthage on the same principle: "I have made it a rule from the beginning of my episcopate not to decide things on my own account without consulting you (the presbyters) and having the agreement of the people..." (Congar, 245).

The practice of consultation declined with the introduction and then gradual domination of a hierarchic, pyramidal model of the church. Although even the late middle ages saw laity participating in ecumenical councils (Kung, 74-92), lay people generally remained passive recipients at the bottom of the pyramid, with the pope and bishops in lonely isolation at the top. By the 19th century, the future Cardinal, John Henry Newman, created an uproar with his now classic essay. "On consulting the Faithful in Matters of Doctrine," in which he argued that, in the fourth century struggle with Arianism, it was the laity and not the bishops who maintained orthodoxy intact.

Vatican II rejected the pyramidal concept of church in favor of a more biblical, communitarian model. It placed the exercise of teaching authority within the context of the church as a community served by that authority. With the rest of the people of God, they are fellow believers, learners, and listeners (GS 44^4).

The existence of rights and obligations in the Church requires that legal structures and mechanisms be set up for the vindication of those rights. The broad pluralistic spectrum of theological opinion existing within the Catholic Church today requires that consultation involve more than one segment of the Church or more that one school of theology. As Cardinal Joseph Ratzinger once acknowledged, "I am convinced that Catholicism's survival depends on our ability to break out of the prison of the Roman-school type" (O'Donovan, 140). A model for wide consultation is that which went into the U.S. Bishops' 1976 Call to Action and their pastoral letters on peace and economic justice.

Canon Law recongnizes the right and duty of the members of the Church to make known to the bishops their opinions on matters pertaining to the good of the church (Canon 212, #3). The responsiblity of the bishops to give serious consideration to those opinions before they teach is left implicit but beyond dispute.

Discussion Questions

It is often said: "The Roman Catholic Church is not a democracy"? Discuss.

How can Catholics best "make known to their leaders their opinions on matters pertaining to the good of the Church"? Make concrete suggestions.

Is the "wide consultation" mentioned in Right 2 practised in your local Church? If not, why not?

Bibliography

1. LG Lumen Gentium. II Vatican Council, Dogmatic Constitution on the Church.

2. HL HUMAN LIFE IN OUR DAY. Pastoral Letter of the U.S. Catholic Bishops. Washington, D.C.: United States Catholic Conference, 1968.

3. DH Dignitatis Humanae. II Vatican Council, Decree on Religious Liberty.

4. GS Gaudium et Spes. II Vatican Council, Pastoral Constitution on the Church.

Yves Congar, O.P. LAY PEOPLE IN THE CHURCH. Westminster, MD: New-man Press, 1965.

Hans Küng, STRUCTURES OF THE CHURCH. New York: Thomas Nelson, 1964.

John Henry Newman, ON CONSULTING THE FAITHFUL IN MATTERS OF DOCTRINE. New York: Sheed & Ward, 1961.

Leo J. O'Donovan, S.J. (ed.), COOPERATION BETWEEN THEOLOGIANS AND THE ECCLESIASTICAL MAGISTERIUM. A report of the Joint Committee of the Canon Law Society of America and the Catholic Theological Society of America. Washington, D.C.: Catholic University of America, 1982.

3. Engaging in Activities

Lawrence S. Cunningham

*All Catholics have the right to engage in any activity which does
not infringe on the rights of others, e.g., they have the right to
freedom of speech, freedom of the press, and freedom of association* (C. 212:2,3, C. 215, C. 223:1).

The key to understanding this right is to be found in the phrase
"which does not infringe on the rights of others." That liberty which is
the liberty of the Children of God most certainly does not include the
liberty to speak, act and associate with those who speak and act against
the basic dignity of others. The right to engage in any activity manifestly
does not give a Catholic the right, say, to be a member of the Ku Klux
Klan or the American Nazi Party.

With that rather obvious caveat in mind we do need to affirm loudly
that Catholics have an inalienable right to speak or act as free persons
even if that speaking or acting is deemed "imprudent" or, in the quaint
jargon of church language, "offensive to pious ears." Whether what is
said or done is in good taste or helpful or desirable is quite another matter. It is the right that needs the emphasis.

An emphasis on that right is important not because the right hasn't
been abused but because the suppression of that right has done incalcul-
able harm to the Church. There is, for example, something monstrous

---

Lawrence S. Cunningham is Professor of Religion at the Florida State
University, Tallahassee, FL.

about those who flog the theories of Teilhard de Chardin now but raised not a finger to help get his theories in print, where they could have been subjected to the rigors of academic scrutiny and public discourse. Whatever fuzziness one might attribute to his thinking can be blamed, in large part, on his inability to get his ideas expressed in a public forum. His case is a microcosm of a problem which only now is being addressed in the Church. The rights under question concern, in short, truth and its accessibility.

It would be nice to think that such basic rights derive directly from the Catholic tradition but, as a quick reading of the *Syllabus of Errors* makes clear, such is not the case. What was required was a shift in thinking about truth as an abstract given, existing in clarity, and fully possessed by the church. If one accepts that notion of truth, then the old dictum that "error has not rights" makes a good deal of sense. The basic rights of which we speak exist in the Catholic Church today because a critical reflection on Enlightenment ideals makes it clear that these rights are not only compatible with the biblical ideal but, at least in part, derive from them. What we have learned is something that Thomas Aquinas understood a long time ago: that our right to have and express the truth falls under the imperative of simple justice; we are due the truth (see S. T. II IIae q. 110). It is only with the slow passage of time that those freedoms (of association, press, speech, etc.) which are at the heart of the liberal democracies came to be recognized as not only in harmony with the authentic Catholic tradition but an aid to its enrichment. To the degree that we possess those rights we are the debtors of those "Americanist" bishops of the last century and thinkers like the late John Courtney Murray in this one who fought to bring them to the fore.

There is a further point.

The great insight of the Second Vatican Council about the pilgrim nature of the Church and its orientation towards the *Eschaton* carries with it the corollary that the Church is, paradoxically, a servant of the truth and in search of the depth of the truth of the Gospel that it has entrusted to it. In the concrete, that means that the working out of the Gospel must be done close to the texture of the experience of those who are the Church, "for we are fellow workers of God, God's field, God's building." (I Cor.3:9). Being called to serve the Gospel does not abrogate our basic human rights; indeed it helps us to affirm our rights as free children of God. Both nature and the Gospel proclaim those rights.

Discussion Questions

1. Can you think of circumstances in which the "good of the Church" would be enhanced by a voluntary self-restriction concerning, say, the right to speak freely in the Church?

2. While everyone would agree that association with Neo-Nazis would not be consonant with the right of association, would you agree that such a right is also restrictive when it would involve the other end of the spectrum (e.g., political groups which are Marxist-Leninist)?

3. Can you name and describe specific instances where your freedom in the sense described above was circumscribed *precisely* because you are a Catholic?

Bibliography

David Hollenbach, CLAIMS IN CONFLICT: RETRIEVING AND RENEWING THE CATHOLIC HUMAN RIGHTS TRADITION. New York: Paulist, 1979.

Hans Küng, TRUTHFULNESS: THE FUTURE OF THE CHURCH. New York: Sheed and Ward, 1968.

4. Access to Information

James Gaffney

All Catholics have the right of access to all information possessed by Church authorities concerning their spiritual and temporal welfare, provided such access does not infringe on the rights of others (C. 218, C. 221: 1, 2, 3, C. 223: 1, C. 537).

The *prima facie* case against the use of secrecy by the Church's officialdom is so plain and striking as to seem at first merely superficially clever. It is, however, absolutely fundamental. As John Henry Newman said, "Revelation is the initial and essential idea of Christianity." We do not have a Church because we believe in God. We have a Church because we believe in a revealing God. And the measure of the Church's authenticity and fidelity is, above all, its service of God precisely as revealing. There is a more than verbal irony in the idea of a concealing Church rendering service to a revealing God. From a theological viewpoint, publicity is essential to the Church and secrecy is, at best, incidental to it. Candor and openness are signs of the Church's health; secretiveness is a symptom of its ailments or a side effect of attempts to cure them.

It is a reflection of this same fundamental aspect of Christianity that we find in the New Testament's frequent, and always positive use of the term for bold, confident, forthright expression, *parrhesia* It is a word

---

James Gaffney is Professor of Ethics at Loyola University, New Orleans, LA.

that had previously taken on great richness of meaning from the social ideals of Greek democracy, as denoting that frankness of communication which properly characterizes discourse, including controversial discourse, among free persons in a free state. No less significant is the same word's other principal context, that of private and personal relationships, where it refers to the typical quality of communication between, or among, friends. The appropriateness of a quality of communication traditionally associated with freedom and friendship can hardly be overlooked by a society founded on such words as "For freedom Christ has set us free" (Gal. 5:1) and "I have called you friends" (Jn. 15:15).

However, even though not itself a virtue, sometimes secrecy is demanded by virtue, occasionally by prudence, most often by fidelity. Candor itself may be possible only on conditions of confidentiality. There are things we want to say, even need to say, which, for excellent reasons, we do not wish to broadcast. In the Church, confessional secrecy has been the most solemn instance of such circumstances. But it is essential to recognize that in such cases information is kept secret for the sake of the very persons who provide it, and on the basis of a clear mutual understanding. Such secrecy is for the sake of facilitating, not impeding communication. It is to insure speech against painful consequences from insensitive, or over-sensitive, or unkind hearers. It is quite different from "state secrecy," to insure operations of government against interference, which, being mainly justifiable as a requirement of military defense or commercial competition, has very little legitimate scope within a Church.

Secrecy becomes an instrument of vice especially when information is withheld in order to maintain power over those who are denied it, or to put them at some practical disadvantage. Insistence on *habeas corpus* in free civil communities exemplifies their recognition of public authority's duty to furnish satisfactory explanations whenever it imposes restraints on freedom. To withhold such explanations is to harass and tyrannize under the pretext of governing, no less in a Church than in a state. Protection from such abuses must include free access to evidence, whether one occupies the position of a plaintiff or that of a defendant in legal disputes (see C. 221).

Again, in a Church no less than in a civil community where freedom is valued, when private resources are used, as often they must be, to serve public interests, those who administer such resources should recognize accountability to those who provide them, if the community is to be protected against not only malfeasance and mismanagement, but also a paternalism that imposes on competent adults conditions appropriate for dependent children. "Holy Mother the Church" may be a defensible metaphor, but even as a metaphor it refers to the Church, not, in any exclusive sense, to the Church's government (see c. 1287.2).

In a modern work that is both conservative and erudite, significantly entitled *The Pathology of Politics*, undue secrecy is wisely diagnosed as one of the outstanding symptoms of a sick civil society. The differences that exist, or are supposed to exist, between a state and a church, are obviously such as to make that diagnosis considerably more applicable to the latter than to the former.

Discussion Questions

1. In what sense is "publicity essential to the Church"? In what sense is it not?

2. What are some historical examples of the practice of secrecy hurting the Church?

3. Is your local Church an open Church?

Bibliography

Sissela Bok, SECRETS: ON THE ETHICS OF CONCEALMENT AND REVELATION. New York: Pantheon, 1983.

Carl Friedrich, THE PATHOLOGY OF POLITICS: VIOLENCE, BETRAYAL, CORRUPTION, SECRECY AND PROPAGANDA. New York: Harper, 1972.

P. Jouon, "Divers sens de PARRHESIA dans le NT," RECHERCHES DE SCIENCES RELIGIEUSES. 30 (1940), pp. 239-241.

5. Choosing Leaders[1]

Hans Küng

All Catholics have the right to a voice in all decisions that affect them, including the choosing of their leaders. (C. 212:3).

People like to talk of the participation of the laity in the *life* (not decisions) of the Church. They also like to speak of the participation of the laity in decisions of the *world* (but not of the Church). They do not at all like to speak, at least in officially binding documents, of the participation of the laity in the *decisions* of the *Church*. Nevertheless it is precisely here that the question of the status of the laity in the Church arises in the most practical way. For, as long as I can contribute advice and work but am excluded from decision-making, I remain, no matter how many fine things are said about my status, a second-class member of this community: I am more an object which is utilized than a subject who is actively responsible. The person who can advise and collaborate but not participate in decision-making in a manner befitting his/her status, is not really the Church but only *belongs* to the Church. Yet this idea contradicts the very understanding of "laity" as we have once again understood it in past decades, not least in Vatican II itself.

The basis for joint decision-making in the Church was itself laid out thoroughly in the Decree on the Apostolate of the Laity of Vatican II, inasmuch as in the first section of the first preparatory chapter it was

Hans Küng is Director of the Institute for Ecumenical Research at Tubingen University, West Germany.

said that the laity "share in the priestly, prophetic, and royal office of
Christ" and that thence they "have their own role to play in the mission
of the whole People of God in the Church and in the world" (Art. 2).
And at the same time the decree alludes to the pertinent section of the
Constitution of the Church because it explains in a concise, beautiful
and constructive way the basis on which our later reflections are
grounded:

> Therefore the chosen People of God is one: "one Lord, one
> faith, one baptism" (Eph. 4:5). As members they share a com-
> mon dignity from their rebirth in Christ. They have the same
> filial grace and the same vocation to perfection. They possess
> in common one salvation, one hope and one undivided charity.
> Hence, there is in Christ and in the Church no inequality on the
> basis of race or nationality, social condition or sex, because
> "there is neither Jew nor Greek; there is neither slave nor
> freeman; there is neither male nor female, for you are all 'one'
> in Christ Jesus" (Gal. 3:28; cf. Col. 3:11).

Now if this is all true—and it is true—then the question arises spon-
taneously: If the community of all those in the Church goes so deep, in
spite of all differences of gifts and services, that it is not possible to go
deeper, then, why considering the communality of the one Lord, of the
one Spirit and the one Body, of one faith and one baptism, of one grace
and vocation, of one hope and love, and finally of one responsibility and
task—why then, despite all the diversity of functions, is there not also in
the Church a communality of *decision?*

The Church, as well as all individuals, remains bound to the basic
witness and service of the original witness without which there would be
no Church. The Church is founded on the apostles (and the prophets).
All the faithful thus are supposed to succeed the apostles in apostolic
faith and confessing, and in service. This service takes the most diverse
forms of proclamation, baptism, the community of prayer and the Supper, the building up of the congregation, and service to the world. The
shepherds in the Church are in no way a management class with unilateral imperial power, toward which the single possible attitude is unilateral obedience. They are not *dominium* but *ministerium*. They form
no power structure but a special service structure. "You know that a-
mong the pagans their so-called rulers lord it over them, and their great
men make their authority felt. This is not to happen among you. No;

anyone who wants to become great among you must be your servant, and anyone who wants to be first among you must be your servant, and anyone who wants to be first among you must be slave to all. For the Son of Man himself did not come to be served but to serve, and to give his life as a ransom for many" (Mark 10:42-45). So the shepherds are *not* the *owners* of the Church, toward whom laity are only dependents who have nothing to say in the management. The Church is not a huge industry: All members of the Church *are* Church, the Church belongs to all of them. And the shepherds are also *not* the *fathers* of the Church, in contrast to whom the laity are only minors who still cannot have any responsibility of their own for the Church. The Church cannot be considered simply as a family (except as under God, the one Father): All grown-up members of the Church are adult members who have an established inalienable responsibility for the whole. And, finally, the shepherds are also *not* the *teachers* of the Church, in contrast to whom the laity are only learning pupils who have only to listen and obey. The Church is not a school: All Church members have "learned from God" (1 Thess. 4:9) and "do not need anyone to teach" them (1 John 2:27).

The joint decision-making of the laity in the Church can obviously *not be founded* on the fact that the fullness of power of the shepherds is derived simply from the fullness of power of the Church or congregation, from the fullness of power of the universal priesthood. Then the special pastoral office would simply be leveled within the Church and within the universal priesthood: an unbiblical democratization!

But on the other hand the participation of the laity in decision-making of the Church can also *not be excluded* on the basis that the fullness of the power of the Church or congregation is simply derived from the fullness of power of the shepherds, as though the shepherds alone stood in succession to the apostles and were not the servants of the Church but its masters or mediators. Thus the pastoral service would be isolated from the Church or congregation, from the universal priesthood, and its apostolic succession would be absolutized: an unbiblical hierarchicalization or clericalization of the Church!

If, however, the Church and her shepherds stand all together under the one Father and Lord, who makes them all brothers and sisters; if they all stand under the one message of Christ and all are called into the same discipleship and the same obedience to God and his Word; if they then ultimately all are the hearing Church and precisely as hearers are all filled with the Spirit, then it follows that the fullness of power of the Church or congregation is not derived from the fullness of power of the shepherds, and the fullness of power of the shepherds is not derived from the fullness of power of Church or congregation, but the fullness of power of *both* is directly derived from the fullness of power of the Lord of the Church in his Spirit. This common origin of their fullness of power establishes the universal authorization of the congregation as well as the special fullness of power of the service of the shepherds. It is the support of the authority of the shepherds as well as of the participation of the "laity" in decision-making.

In conclusion let us say only this: Obviously there is no perfect system of organization; in concrete life each has its specific defects and dangers. But a system better than that canonized by the Code of Canon Law is not difficult to think of! Participatory decision-making corresponds better both to the original organization of the apostolic Church and to our own contemporary democratic times. What was originally correct cannot later on be rejected as false in principle by those who call themselves followers.

Discussion Questions

1. What is the biblical and traditional precedence for shared decision-making in the Church?

2. What areas of Church life would be open to shared decision-making and what areas would not?

3. The current centralized control model of the Church is the result particularly of past abuses which developed in the participatory model (lay investiture, politically-controlled offices, nepotism, etc.). What sort of practical model could be developed in the Church today to enable all the People of God to exercise their shared priestly, prophetic and royal offices in the life of the Church while guarding against past problems?

Bibliography

Barbara A. Cullom and Richard C. Dieter, eds., NOT SERVANTS BUT FRIENDS. Quixote Center, P.O. Box 5206, Hyattsville, MD 20782, 1985.

John L. McKenzie, AUTHORITY IN THE CHURCH. Sheed & Ward, P.O. Box 414292, Kansas City, MO 64141, 1966.

Leonardo Boff, CHURCH: CHARISM & POWER. The Crossroad Publishing Co., 370 Lexington Ave. New York, NY 10017, 1985.

Note

1. Excerpted, at the suggestion of the author, from his "Participation Of The Laity In Church Leadership And Elections" in SIGNPOSTS FOR THE FUTURE. Garden City, N.Y.: Doubleday, 1978.

6. Accountability of Leaders

Daniel C. Maguire

All Catholics have the right to have their leaders accountable to them. (C. 492, C. 1287.2).

To be accountable, according to the *Oxford English Dictionary*, is to be "liable to be called to answer for responsibilities and conduct." Accountability is a foundational moral concept; it is a predicate of our essential sociality. Humanity is a shared glory and we are answerable to all those who share it with us. Accountability is the first-born child of justice. Justice tells us that we are not an island, that the common good which is the setting of all private good is something for which we are, one and all, accountable.

The accountability addressed in this article is that of Church leaders. Christianity introduced a revolution in the concept of both leadership and accountability. These are the words of Jesus, according to Mark: "You know that in the world the recognized rulers lord it over their subjects, and their great men make them feel the weight of authority. This is not the way with you; among you, whoever wants to be great must be your servant, and whoever wants to be first must be the willing slave of all" (Mark 10: 42-43). Scholars such as C. H. Dodd judge that this model of authority traces back to the mind of Jesus and that for Jesus it was "fundamental to the whole idea of the divine commonwealth."[1] The models that Jesus offers to those who would be leaders in the com-

---

Daniel Maguire is Professor of theology at Marquette University, Milwaukee, WI.

munity are the child, the lackey, and the slave, none of which even had legal standing in the contemporary society. This radical re-imagining of authority resonates faithfully in the lexicon of the Christian scriptures. These scriptures know the contemporary words for office-holders (*arche, time, telos*), but avoid them and coin a new word *diakonia* (service) to describe Church leadership. It uses those other terms only to refer to synagogic and governmental officers.

The Jesus revolution in the notion of authority, therefore, also transformed the notion of accountability. No leaders are to be more accountable than Christian leaders. This was the primeval Christian ideal.

History and sin were, as ever, unkind to the ideal. By the fifth century, Pope Leo I was claiming a "*plenitudo potestatis*," thus mimicking the claims of the Roman imperial dictatorship. This claim implied a "divine right" to lord it over everyone else and it eliminated accountability. As Walter Ullmann says, "this papal plentitude of power was . . . a thoroughly juristic notion and could be understood only . . . against the Roman law background."[2] That background tendentially or explicitly deified the Emperor, leaving no conceptual grounds for accountability.

This authoritarian poison still pollutes manifestations of Catholic leadership and must be countered by calls for accountability. Catholic theology teaches that misused authority has no moral weight. As Suarez said, "one is under no obligation to obey" the pope when "he abuses his power against justice and the common good."[3] Authority that does not accept accountability serves neither justice nor the common good, and therefore lacks moral standing.

Church leaders should be accountable to all members of the Church in 1) their public teaching and policies; 2) their coordination of the various Christian ministries; and 3) in administering the finances of the Church. In none of these areas is a pope or a bishop a "corporation sole." Such a model would be an elementary rejection of the Gospel ideal.

Given the historical tendency of Church leaders to follow the Leonine claim of a "plenitude of power," accountability might best be guaranteed by new laws which limit the terms of Church leaders, broaden the base of their election, and provide for more accessible procedures of impeachment. The hierarchical record of financial and spiritual accountability to all Catholics has not been uniformly edifying. Major reforms that go well beyond Vatican II are urgently needed.

Discussion Questions

1. Discuss the problem of the ownership of Church properties and Church monies. Is there any model for accountablity in modern life, or is this unique?

2. In what ways is the current hierarchical Church compatible/incompatible with the Gospel ideal of authority as service?

3. What specific changes could make the Catholic hierarchy more accountable in every way?

Bibliography

Leonardo Boff, CHURCH, CHARISM AND POWER: LIBERATION THEOLOGY AND THE INSTITUTIONAL CHURCH. New York: Crossroad, 1985.

Albert Nolan, JESUS BEFORE CHRISTIANITY. Maryknoll: Orbis, 1978.

Vincent J. Donovan, CHRISTIANITY REDISCOVERED. Maryknoll: Orbis, 1982.

Notes

1. C. H. Dodd, THE FOUNDER OF CHRISTIANITY (New York: Macmillan, 1970), p. 93.

2. Walter Ullman, A SHORT HISTORY OF THE PAPACY IN THE MIDDLE AGES (London: Methuen, 1972), p. 220.

3. F. Suarez, DE FIDE THEOLOGICA, Disputatio X de Summo Pontifice, Sectio VI, OPERA OMNIA (Paris: 1858), pp. 12, 318.

7. Voluntary Associations

Rosemary Radford Ruether

All Catholics have the right to form voluntary associations to pursue Catholic aims, including the right to worship together; such associations have the right to decide on their own rules of governance. (C. 215, C. 299, C. 300, C. 305, C. 309).

The right of Catholics to voluntary associations, including associations for worship, derives both from the nature of human community and from the nature of the Church as a spiritual community. Human communities are formed by the free and voluntary consent of persons to enter into a covenant together. This is true of marriage, which is valid only when both partners freely consent to the relationship. It is also true of civil society where the validity of government derives from the consent of the governed. Consent to enter into community implies a participation by all members in decision-making at some level and a social relationship intended to be just and beneficial to all.

Human communities lose their validity to the extent to which structures of social relationship are forced upon some members by others, without their consent, and kept in place by coercive power. This is particularly true when systems of coercion are enforced for the purpose of giving a monopoly on power and the benefits of the material resources of the society to the few by exploiting the labor of the many.

Rosemary Radford Ruether is Georgia Harkness Professor of Applied Theology at Garrett-Evangelical Theological Seminary, Evanston, IL.

The Church as a spiritual community is essentially a voluntary association. It is intended to be paradigmatic of authentic human community as a free, just and participatory society. The very nature of the Spirit which forms and sustains the Church is freedom. The Spirit "blows where it wills" and creates, by its nature, a free, non-coercive community, whose members gather in mutual delight to love and serve one another.

Although the Church necessarily also takes on the character of a historical institution, perpetuating itself by laws and organizational structures, it can never lose the element of free, voluntary association. Christians remain free to form new voluntary communities and associations on local, regional, national and international levels to express new social needs and visions. Recognition of areas of injustice, such as the oppression of women, of one race by another, or of industrial workers, are appropriate occasions to create new associations to give particular attention to these concerns. Such associations recontextualize the vision of redemption of the gospel in each new historical period. Voluntary associations thus are manifestations of the ongoing presence of the Spirit in the Church.

Included in such rights to voluntary association are gatherings for worship outside the regular parish structure, in the context of free, intentional communities. Such gatherings are particularly appropriate to express the prayer-life of groups bonded together around particular commitments. It can be from such experimental worship gatherings that the renewal of liturgy can spring. Such gatherings are freer than the parish community to be experimental. Such experimental liturgical communities can be particularly helpful in expressing in new forms of worship new developments of social consciousness. One example of this today is feminist liturgical communities. Recognizing the long tradition in the Church of androcentric language and religious symbols and the exclusion of women from participation in ministry, such gatherings can experiment with new symbols and forms of worship that repent of and heal women and men from the tradition of sexism and affirm the full personhood of women.

It is essential that such new developments in worship be in dialogue with the larger historical Church. This means a free dialogue in which voluntary communities of prayer pursue their inspiration fully, according to their own understanding, but also communicate their creative work through publication, demonstration or other channels of conversation, with other Christians outside their particular group. In this way the new social consciousness of such experimental communites, and new liturgical symbols which express such new consciousness in worship, inform and leaven the historical Church. Therefore voluntary communities and associations should not be seen by the historical Church, or come to see themselves, as separatist or sectarian, but rather as a necessary catalyst for developments of consciousness, worship and social practice for the whole Church. The historical Church is renewed to the extent that it is open to the authentic developments in such communities and is able to receive the creative work that develops in such voluntary gatherings into its ongoing life.

Discussion Questions

1. What are the primary causes among Catholics today for the formation of voluntary associations and extra-parochial worship communities?

2. What are the major problems or conflicts between such groups and the received Catholic understanding of the Church?

3. How can a positive relationship between voluntary communities and the historical Church best be facilitated?

Bibliography

Leonardo Boff, CHURCH, CHARISM AND POWER: A RADICAL ECCLESIOLOGY. New York: Crossroads, 1985.

Rosemary Ruether, WOMAN-CHURCH: THEOLOGY AND PRACTICE OF FEMINIST LITURGICAL COMMUNITIES. San Francisco: Harper and Row, 1986.

Sergio Torres, THE CHALLENGE OF BASIC CHRISTIAN COMMUNITIES. Maryknoll, New York: Orbis Books, 1981.

8. Expressing Dissent

Joseph Koury, SJ

All Catholics have the right to express publicly their dissent in regard to decisions made by Church authorities. (C. 212:3, C.218, C. 753)

Let me state my findings: There is no expression in the documents of Vatican II or in any magisterial document known to me, of a right to dissent enjoyed by all Catholics, nor of a right to express dissent publicly. However, that is not to say that the possibility of legitimate dissent from non-definitive teaching, and/or publicly expressed dissent, in particular cases, is excluded. On the contrary, theological manuals in widespread use prior to Vatican II recognized that possibility, and the bishops assembled at Vatican II corrected, improved upon, and in some cases dissented from non-infallible teachings of prior pontiffs and councils. In fact, there is much discussion in both theological and magisterial texts of the possibility, condition, legitimacy, and consequences of dissent and public expression of dissent from non-infallible doctrine.

To exclude the possibility of dissent would be tantamount to denying the meaning and uses of those distinctions constantly employed by popes, councils, and theologians, such as dogma, doctrine, opinion; ordinary and extraordinary magisterium; universal and particular magisterium (e.g., canons 749, 750, 752, 753). It would be to homogenize the

---

Joseph Koury, SJ, is Associate Professor of Canon Law at the Weston School of Theology, Weston, MA.

different kinds of responses from the faithful called for by the different nature and content of magisterial documents. Different documents and their content oblige differently; thus, the *Code of Canon Law,* officially promulgated legislation for the Latin Church, which binds seriously, is not a dogmatic text, except as it contains dogmas previously defined. Obligations differ, e.g., "religious submission of will and mind," "due respect for the magisterium," and "must be believed with divine and catholic faith" illustrate the variety of ways in which the Church expressly obligates the faithful (e.g., canons 218, 750, 752, 753).

To exclude the possibility of dissent to non-infallible teaching would have the effect of saying that the Church only responds to moral or doctrinal questions in its "highest," most authoritative and most binding exercise of teaching authority; or, failing that, no response. On the contrary, in all that has not been defined *de fide,* the Church, for the guidance of the faithful, must be able to "draw nearer to the truth," and in the process must be able to give provisional but authoritative and variously-binding teachings. The authoritative, but non-definitive, teaching of popes and councils is that the legitimate exercise of authoritative but not definitive teaching authority is binding upon Catholics, but not in the same way that a dogmatic authoritative definitive teaching is binding. There cannot but be a "hierarchy of truths" in what the Church teaches, a hierarchy in the way it teaches and in the manner in which it means to obligate the responses of the faithful to those truths.

That the hierarchical and theological magisteria employ such distinctions is incontrovertible, as are the controversies that surround the meanings of such distinctions.

The Firm Tradition: "Divisions Of Opinion"

What we today call "differences of opinion," which sometimes overflow into dissent, encyclopedias and history books call theological controversies and disputes. These are characteristic of the Church, even from its beginning. Peter justified to the "circumcisers among the brethren" how he could eat with the uncircumcised (Acts 11: 1-18). Paul and Barnabas confronted "the party of the Pharisees" among the apostles and elders who held to the necessity of circumcision of the Gentiles and the imposition of the law of Moses (Acts 15:1-35).

A mendicant-order teacher, Aquinas was suspect to his secular clergy masters at the University of Paris. His Aristotelian philosophy, pagan in origin and transmitted by infidels, was refuted by Platonists. In 1277, the Bishop of Paris condemned fifteen propositions related to Thomas' teachings; this condemnation was not formally revoked until two years after Thomas' canonization. Four centuries later, Erasmus, scripture scholar and humanist, was offered a cardinal's hat by Pope Paul III, but his writings were listed in the *Index of Forbidden Books* by the Council of Trent. Theological controversies surrounded Robert Bellarmine, cardinal and archbishop. His theory of indirect papal power in secular affairs was too cautious for one pope, too papal for several secular rulers; his writings were nearly listed on the *Index* (the death of the pope in 1570 saved him). He was caught up in the controversies on efficacious grace, and, in 1616, he delivered the Holy See's admonition of Galileo. He was named a doctor of the church four centuries later.

In this century, theologians (among them, John Courtney Murray) who were silenced as teachers or writers, were later rehabilitated, and some, invited as experts at Vatican II.

Notable examples, then, of the firm tradition of "division of opinion" involves apostles and elders, university professors and bishops, "schools" and "systems," cardinals and popes. A sampling of forms of disputes and dialogue would include verbal, pedagogical, written, personal, and their diverse content: pastoral and liturgical practices, courses of instruction, theological, doctrinal and religio-political matters. Various attempts at resolution: a hearing at the "Jerusalem council," approvals and disapprovals, *Index* and admonition. But there is one constant thread: The expression of differences of theological opinion within the one "community of believers," is evidence, it seems to me, of the interaction of magisteria in the Church.

A Useful Principle

Despite later efforts to restrict it, a principle enunciated by Pope Pius IX in 1923 remains useful:

> In those matters in which there is division of opinion among the best authors in Catholic schools, no one is to be forbidden to follow that opinion which seems to him [or her] to be nearer the truth (*AAS* 15 (1923), 307f; transl. *Canon Law Digest* 1 (1934), 669-70).

The specific task of theology is "faith seeking understanding" and, I would add, practice. Inevitably, in the task of bringing new expression to "timeless truths of faith," in penetrating the mysteries of faith, there will be disagreement in the expression of opinion, which only reinforces the need for dialogue.

Therefore, it is not surprising that there are canons in the revised *Code of Canon Law* that point, however obliquely, to this long tradition of "division of opinions."

Not in so many words do we find the expression of a right to dissent. Yet, even given the limitations attached to the listing of certain rights, one can hardly exclude *a priori* the possibility of dissent, as when the *Code* states that the Christian faithful have the "right and even at times the duty to manifest to the sacred pastors their opinion on matters which pertain to the good of the Church, and a right to make known their opinion to other Christian faithful" (c. 212, § 3)˙ Again, even given the restriction "while observing a due respect for the magisterium of the Church," one can hardly rule out the possibility of dissent and the public expression of dissent in the exercise of the "lawful freedom of inquiry and of prudently expressing their opinions on matters in which they have expertise" (c. 218) which those engaged in sacred disciplines enjoy. Even the obligation of obedience to "follow what the sacred pastors, as representatives of Christ, declare as teachers of the faith or determine as leaders of the church": (c. 212, § 1) does not absolutely foreclose on the possibility of dissent. For, what governs all this is the Church's recognition of the right and obligation which all persons enjoy to seek, embrace and observe the truth (canon 748, § 1).

While there is no magisterial statement which expressly names the right to dissent or to dissent publicly, so also there is no magisterial teaching absolutely denying such a right or stating the impossibility of dissent. To my knowledge, no pope or council has declared definitively, infallibly exercising their teaching authority, as it a dogma of faith that dissent in the Church is absolutely not possible, or that public dissent is absolutely not permitted. What is not absolutely forbidden may be permitted.

Discussion Questions

1. Is the statement of a right and even at times a duty to manifest one's opinion, and/or the right of freedom of inquiry and prudent expression of opinion, equivalent to a right to dissent publicly?

2. How do you distinguish disagreement, dissent, disobedience?

3. What are the implications of the historical evidence of both continuity and discontinuity in the development and teaching of doctrine?

Bibliography

Francis Sullivan, MAGISTERIUM: TEACHING AUTHORITY IN THE CATHOLIC CHURCH. Paulist Press, 1983. Clear, accurate presentation of distinctions often overlooked. Scattered throughout the book are references to assent/dissent.

Ladislas Orsy, "Reflections on the Text of a Canon," AMERICA, May 17, 1986, 396-99. While his focus is C. 752 of the 1983 CODE, Orsy explores the meanings of distinctions used in magisterial texts, and the kinds of responses called for by such documents.

Charles Curran, FAITHFUL DISSENT. Sheed & Ward, 1986. Especially valuable reading is Chapter 2, which discusses the theological issues. Part 2: Documentation provides a number of previously unpublished texts.

9. Administrative and Judicial Procedures

Paul L. Golden, CM

All Catholics have the right to be dealt with according to commonly accepted norms of fair administrative and judicial procedures without undue delay. (C.221: 1, 2, 3, C. 223, 1, 2)

The effective protection of all human rights is a concern of the governments of nations and for the Church itself. (Vatican II, *Dignitas Humanae* #1). The effective protection of ecclesial rights is a particular concern of the Church and is addressed in Right #9. Catholics have the right to juridical and administrative procedures which provide adequate protection and vindication of ecclesial rights. These procedures are known as due process.

The Church has always accepted responsibility for settling disputes between its members, particularly when these disputes are between private individuals and groups in the Church (Mt. 18:15-18). This has been part of the Church's healing and reconciling ministry. Even when the Church was still under the influence of the Roman Empire, it employed processes and structures to hear and resolve conflicts. From the twelfth century until the reform of Pius X, administrative acts as well as judicial

---

Paul Golden, CM, is a Director of the Institute for Leadership of Religious Organizations at DePaul University, Chicago, IL, and President of the Canon Law Society of America.

decisions could be appealed by an aggrieved party to the tribunal of one's metropolitan See or to the Roman Rota. The 1917 Code of Canon Law contained a full judicial process. Provisions were made for an independent judiciary, the right of an individual to be represented by an advocate, the right to a speedy trial, the right to an appeal and other such protections. This Code also had a canon on administrative recourse (C. 1667), but the process was rudimentary and wholly inadequate.

Due process is a term which comes from the Anglo-American legal tradition. This tradition requires that, substantively, no fundamental right or freedom be denied without appropriate justification and, procedurally, that each person be given certain protections when his/her rights are challenged or questioned in administrative or juridical process. Examples of such procedural protections are: the right to be informed of proposed actions which might be prejudicial to one's rights, the right to be heard in defense of one's rights, the right to confront one's accusers and the right not to be judged by one's accusers.

The Church's juridical forum has historically been used almost exclusively for cases involving the validity of the marriage bond. The juridical procedure found in the revised Code of Canon Law (CC. 1400-1670), while updated, has not substantially changed. While some canonists discuss a wider use of this process, it will probably remain limited to marriage cases in the near future.

Experience has shown, however, that it is the discretionary use of administrative authority which more often results in the denial of rights and the beginning of conflicts. In 1969, to fill this gap in adequate procedures to protect rights, the National Conference of Catholic Bishops adopted a set of conciliation and arbitration procedures which were formulated by a committee of the Canon Law Society of America. This document was ratified by the Holy See in 1971. Today, most of the dioceses in the United States have in place some form of due process modeled on this document.

In this model, due process has a three-fold structure. The first is conciliation. When two parties are in conflict, they agree to the conciliation services of a third party who attempts to bring the parties to an agreement. The second structure is arbitration. The parties to a dispute agree to be bound by the decisions of an arbitrator who has examined all the available facts. The third structure calls for the creation of administrative tribunals whose decisions do not need the voluntary agreement of the parties in order to be binding.

Influenced by the experience of due process, the revised Code also contains norms for recourse against administrative authority (CC. 1732-1752). Administrative authority is that power of governance which executes the law, especially by applying it to local situations. Sometimes this requires interpreting the law, making decrees, dispensing from the law and even applying certain penalties. Administrative action requires the exercise of discretion. In order to avoid arbitrary and unjust decisions administrative discretion should be structured. Such a structure should include: 1) documents specifying the competence of all who exercise authority; 2) written and published policies which guide the decisions to be made; and 3) written reasoned opinions which support administrative decisions and can be used to guide future decisions.

Right #9 also mentions that Catholics have a right to these procedures without undue delay. This seems to have greater application in connection with the next right on the redress of grievances. Suffice it to repeat here the words of the sage jurist: "Justice delayed is justice denied."

Discussion Questions

1. The new pastor unilaterally disbands the parish council. He announces that he does not need the advice of the council and he considers it a waste of time. The council has been an effective group for over ten years and the members of the parish are angry. Does the pastor have a right to do this? Are the people's rights violated? Is there any recourse?

2. The principal of the parish grade school has received two years of favorable evaluations from the pastor. This year he announces to her that he will not renew her contract. When she asks why she is being let go, he only says that he has other plans for the school. Rumor has it that he will hire a friend of his as the new principal. Do you think her rights are being violated? Which rights? What can she do?

Bibliography

John Beal. "Protecting the Rights of Lay Catholics," THE JURIST 47 (1987), pp. 129-164.

Robert Kennedy, "Address on Due Process to the NCCB," CLSA PROCEEDINGS 31 (1969), 10-17.

Adam Maida, "Rights in the Church," CHICAGO STUDIES 15 (1976), pp. 255-267.

National Catholic Conference of Bishops, ON DUE PROCESS, rev. ed. Washington, D.C.: NCCB, 1972.

"Promoting and Protecting Rights in the Church," THE JURIST 46 (1986), pp. 1-342.

10. Redress of Grievances

John M. Huels, O.S.M.

All Catholics have the right to redress of grievances through regular procedures of law. (C. 221: 1, 2, 3, C. 223: 1, 2)

The right to redress grievances in the Church can be traced to Jesus himself who said that conflicts involving his followers which cannot be resolved between themselves should be arbitrated by witnesses or referred to the community for judgment (Mt. 18:15-18). St. Paul wrote that Christians should not bring cases against one another to civil court, but conflicts should be judged within the Church (I Cor. 6:1-6). Already in the second century the Church had a developing judicial system for resolving disputes. By the early third century there is evidence of a well established judicial system, as seen in the *Disdiscalia Apostolorum*, with its detailed regulations on Church court procedures and requirements of the bishop-judge. In the fourth century the Roman emperor Constantine granted to bishops civil power to judge cases. This contributed to the great influences of Roman civil law on ecclesiastical courts which is still evident today. From the Middle Ages until the early twentieth century, aggrieved parties could appeal both administrative acts and judicial decisions to their metropolitan tribunal or to the Roman Rota, but in 1908 Pius X limited administrative recourse against decisions of a bishop to the congregations of the Roman curia.

John Huels, O.S.M., is Associate Professor of Canon Law at the Catholic Theological Union, Chicago, IL.

The right of Christians to redress of grievances through regular procedures of law is enunciated in canon 221 of the 1983 Code of Canon Law. There are chiefly three ways that this right may be vindicated: through diocesan mediation boards, hierarchic recourse, or Church courts.

When conflicts cannot be resolved privately between persons, the law recommends that the parties attempt a solution through mediation or arbitration before taking a case to court (canons 1446, 1713-1716). The law permits national conferences of bishops to establish norms regulating diocesan mediation boards (canon 1733,2). In the United States diocesan mediation boards have existed since 1971. Unfortunately, they are underutilized because the faithful are largely unaware of their existence or of their great potential for redressing grievances.

A second way to redress a grievance in the Church is by hierarchic recourse (canons 1732-1739) whereby an aggrieved party petitions a Church official for the review of an act or decision of a lower administrator. For example, a mother believes that her child's right to receive Confirmation is being denied by the pastor. If she cannot resolve the dispute with the pastor, and either party does not wish to submit the case to a diocesan mediation board, she can make recourse to the bishop, and if she is aggrieved by his decision, she can make recourse again to an appropriate congregation of the Roman curia.

The law also provides the possibility for administrative tribunals to handle cases resulting from an act of administrative power (canon 1400,-2), but proposed new canons on administrative tribunals were eliminated from the final version of the Code promulgated by John Paul II. Unless dioceses establish their own administrative tribunals, a rather serious deficiency in the right to redress grievances will continue because judicial tribunals lack competence to deal with controversies arising from an act of administrative power.

The third principal way of seeking redress of grievances is through the judicial system of the Church. Anyone, even those not baptized, can be a party to an ecclesiastical trial (canon 1476). The object of a trial is to prosecute or vindicate rights, declare juridic facts, or penalize offenses (canon 1400, 1). The party who feels aggrieved by the sentence of the first instances court has the right of appeal to the metropolitan or other designated court. If the two sentences are discordant, the case can then be appealed to the Roman Rota.

Among the problems related to procedural law in the Church are:
(1) widespread ignorance about ecclesiastical procedures and insufficient canon lawyers available to act as counsel in disputes; (2) a lack of clarity, even by canonists, on how administrative cases are handled, since the procedures and decisions of the Roman congregations are rarely published; (3) the lack of diocesan administrative tribunals and the lack of an intermediary authority for hierarchic recourse between the bishop and the Holy See; (4) the burden of so many marriage nullity cases which make Church tribunals practically unavailable for the resolution of other cases. Thus, while the right of redress of grievances is, and has always been, an important value in the Church, some serious difficulties stand in the way of an adequate exercise of this right for many, if not most, members of the Church.

Discussion Questions

1. A new pastor announces to his parishioners on Sunday that he is going to remove all the kneelers from the church because he believes kneeling is inappropriate at Mass. Many parishioners, including members of the parish council, are upset and ask him if he would reconsider, but he refuses. What options do they have now?

2. Do you know of any cases in which two Catholics or a group of Catholics had a serious disagreement over some matter in the Church which they could not resolve among themselves. How was the case handled? Was there any attempt to seek the interventions of higher Church authority?

Bibliography

The Canon Law Society of America Permanent Seminar. PROMOTING AND PROTECTING RIGHTS IN THE CHURCH. Studies by canonists and others published in THE JURIST 46 (1986).

See especially the commentaries on rights by James H. Provost (pages 119-173) and on procedural law by Lawrence G. Wrenn (pages 943-1022). James A. Coriden, Thomas J. Green, Donald E. Heintschel eds., THE CODE OF CANON LAW: A TEXT AND COMMENTARY. New York: Paulist Press, 1985.

William Bassett and Peter Huizing eds., JUDGMENT IN THE CHURCH. CONCILIUM, vol. 107. New York: Seabury Press, 1977.

11. Good Reputations

Anita Kaspery, IHM

All Catholics have the right not to have their good reputations impugned or their privacy violated. (C.220)

It is the purpose of this brief paper to show the relationship of the above Article to Canon 220 in the Revised Code of Canon Law, to give some background with regard to these rights in the Catholic tradition, especially in modern times, and to discuss the appropriateness of this article in the Charter. The last point will conclude with remarks on the pertinence of this article at the present historical moment in the Church.

Canon 220 in the Revised Code reads: "No one is permitted to damage unlawfully the good reputation which another person enjoys or to violate the right of another person to protect his or her own privacy." The Commentary on the Code remarks that this Canon is expressed "in a passive manner."[1] Certainly the wording in the Charter is stronger and more positive, placing emphasis on the possession of these rights rather than on the offender who might seek to usurp them.

The history of the development of human rights theory in the Church can receive only truncated treatment here. Suffice it to say that the most complete list of human rights in the modern Catholic tradition appears

---

Anita Caspary, IHM, is former president of the Immaculate Heart community in Los Angeles and Professor of Literature in the program of Feminist Spirituality at Immaculate Heart College Center, Los Angeles.

in *Pacem in Terris* (1963) where the right of Catholics "to one's good reputation" is stated. The right to "freedom of communication" mentioned in the same document can be interpreted as the right to privacy, applied more narrowly.[2]

To *Pacem in Terris* is given the accolade of "the central and classical document for the doctrine of human rights in the Roman Catholic tradition."[3] It provides a "basis for the transformation of Catholicism from an ally and ward of traditionalist regimes to a critic of both reactionary and revolutionary regimes."[4]

The document "The Church in the Modern World" from Vatican II includes in its list of rights both the right to a good name and the right to privacy, basing all human rights on "the sublime dignity of the human person."[5] The revised Code of Canon Law, as previously noted, incorporates these rights, but, as the Commentary points out, they "preexist the law for they arise from human nature."[6]

If these rights "pre-exist" the law, why are they given a place in the Code or in the Charter? Clearly, they are not rights meant exclusively for Catholics. But the Christian faith does endow them with a "second explicitly Christian warrant from the principle of human dignity."[7] This warrant rests on the belief that all persons are created in the image of God, redeemed by Jesus Christ, and called by God to a destiny beyond history. This belief "supports and interprets the fundamental significance of human nature."[8] Thus the Christian insight deepens the sense of responsibility of each human being for all others, the sense of protection for the rights of others, beyond the care native to human beings for each other.

Another reason for including the right to good reputation and the right to privacy in the Charter is an educational one. For most Catholics the Code of Canon Law remains a closed book, with little application to their daily lives except in extraordinary personal circumstances. The Charter, with less juridic language, makes these rights accessible to all Catholics.

Lastly, these rights have a place in the Charter by reason of the network of human community found in Scripture. A succinct description of the "People of God" and their co-responsibility for human rights is given in "The Church in the Modern World," from Vatican II, No. 32. Here is described the covenant made by God with his people and the confirmation of that covenant in the coming of Jesus. The Word made flesh shared human fellowship in his interaction with neighbors and friends, with publicans and sinners. In his preaching, he emphasized the obligation of all the people of God to treat each other as brothers and sisters. His ultimate test, made vivid by his own death, was to say, "Greater love has no man than this, that a man lay down his life for his friends"[9] (John 15:13). "God's love for the world and the love exemplified and realized in Jesus Christ are important elements in the conception of human love which is ethically normative for Christians."[10] These scriptural examples justify the concern each member of the Christian community has, in love, for each other. Certainly there should be major concern for the reputation and privacy of each.

The spirit of Vatican II has lately suffered severe retrenchment. The reassertion of the rights and dignity of humankind by the Association for the Rights of Catholics is a cry of protest lest the impact of Vatican II and the revised Code be lost in the course of human history.

Because this is a day of rapid and international communication through a variety of media, and because the Church has attained a high degree of visibility, reports of criticism and censure visited upon individuals or groups by the Church easily become threats to good reputation. While at times privacy may keep injustices hidden, individuals should retain this right while under censure. Neither past faithful service of the Church nor pledges of continued fidelity have stopped this seemingly endless series of unhappy events affecting both reputation and privacy.[11]

A change of hierarchical policy can take place only when the rank and file of Catholics openly protest the injustices done to persons who are being robbed of their rights to good reputation and privacy. The thrust of Vatican II toward an open, dialogic loving community may well be forgotten in the present tension. By reiterating the right to a good name and the right to privacy, and by explanations of these and other rights, the Association for the Right of Catholics in the Church will fulfill the purpose of its establishment and give new hope to those discouraged by the present situation.

Discussion Questions

1. Is there a distinction between human rights and the rights of Catholics in the Church? Use examples for illustration.

2. Name some recent instances in which the right to a good reputation has been impugned. Have any measures been taken to correct the injustice of these instances?

3. Is there any instance in the gospels which shows Jesus observed this right?

Bibliography

James A Coriden, Thomas J. Green, Donald E. Heintschel, eds. THE CODE OF CANON LAW: A TEXT AND COMMENTARY. New York: The Paulist Press, 1985.

David Hollenbach, CLAIMS IN CONFLICT, New York: The Paulist Press, 1979.

Charles E. Curran, and Richard A. McCormick, SJ, READINGS IN MORAL THEOLOGY, No. 5. New York: The Paulist Press, 1986.

Foreign Language Bibliography:

Franz Greiner, "Der Laie: seine Pflichte und Rechte," INTERNATIONALE KATHOLISCHE ZEITSCHRIFT: COMMUNIO 14:5 (Sept. 1985), pp. 432-37.

Matthew Kaiser, HANDBUCH DES KATHOLISCHEN KIRCHENRECHTE. 1983.

K. Morsdorf, "Persona in Ecclesia Christi," ARCHIV FUR KATHOLISCHES KIRCHENRECHT 131 (1962).

Notes

1. James H. Provost, "The Obligations and Rights of all the Christian Faithful," THE CODE OF CANON LAW: A TEXT AND COMMENTARY, Book II, Part I, James A. Coriden, Thomas J. Green, and Donald E. Heintschel, eds., (New York: Paulist Press, 1985), p. 153.

2. PACEM IN TERRIS, Nos. 11-27.

3. John Langen, SJ, "Human Rights in Roman Catholicism," READINGS IN MORAL THEOLOGY, No. 5, Charles E. Curran and Richard A. McCormick, SJ, eds., (New York: Paulist Press, 1986), p. 110.

4. Ibid.

5. No. 26, VATICAN COUNCIL II: THE CONCILIAR & POST-CONCILIAR DOCUMENTS, Austin Flannery, ed., (Northport, New York: Costello Publishing Co., 1975), p. 927.

6. James H. Provost, op. cit., p. 139.

7. David Hollenbach, SJ, "Global Human Rights," READINGS IN MORAL THEOLOGY, No. 5, p. 376.

8. Ibid.

9. VATICAN COUNCIL II, op. cit. pp. 931-2.

10. David Hollenbach, SJ, CLAIMS IN CONFLICT (New York: Paulist Press, 1979), p. 108.

11. Examples of this trend are found in the threat of dismissal from their religious communities of the signers of an ad in the NEW YORK TIMES who urged theological

dialogue; the dismissal of a scholar-priest from the ranks of Roman Catholic theologians; the investigation of bishops, seminaries, and religious orders; the taking over of much of his jurisdiction over his archdiocese of a dedicated archbishop; the insistence of a choice between membership in their communities and public service put to several religious.

12a. Ministries for a Christian Life

Charles Curran

All Catholics have the right to receive from the Church those ministries which are needed for the living of a fully Christian life, including:

(a) Instruction in the Catholic tradition and the presentation of moral teaching in a way that promotes the helpfulness and relevance of Christian values to contemporary life. (C. 229: 1, 2)

What we call Christianity or the Church was often called The Way in the Acts of the Apostles (e.g., 9:2). Jesus is the way, the truth and the life. The followers of Jesus are called to live a life of discipleship in the Christian community.

The entire Church community has a role to play in understanding the Catholic tradition and in communicating the moral dimensions of the gospel response in the light of the changing circumstances of time and place. The Constitution on the Church of Vatican II (par. 12) recognizes that through baptism all members of the Church share in the prophetic or teaching function of Jesus just as they share in the priestly role of Jesus. In addition, special charisms or gifts are given to individuals to

---

Charles Curran is a priest of the diocese of Rochester and teaches Roman Catholic Moral Theology at Cornell University, Ithaca, NY.

carry out a specifically prophetic role in the Christian community. Some in the Church community through their scholarly skills devote their lives to the study of scripture and theology. Parents have a specific teaching function with regard to their children. Many people also serve as teachers both in the informal realities of human existence and in more structured programs of catechesis and training both for adults and children.

A special teaching office in the Roman Catholic Church is given to the pope and bishops. The faithful owe the assent of faith to the infallible hierarchical teaching and the religious respect of intellect and will to authoritative non-infallible teaching. (CC. 749-752). History indicates how the hierarchical teaching function has evolved and changed over the years and centuries. For example, the very name and manner of functioning of the papal magisterium in moral matters, as we know it today, are quite recent in church history.

The object or content of these various moral teaching roles in the Church is the entire Christian moral life. The scriptures remind us that the fundamental call of the gospel is to conversion and change of heart (Mk. 1:15). Continual conversion must characterize the life of all Christians. Moral teaching and education must emphasize the call to conversion, the discipleship in the community of the Church, the dispositions that should characterize the Christian person, the values that should mark Christian life, as well as the morality of particular actions.

Within the Christian community moral teaching should take place in a variety of ways. The liturgy is a central and very important teaching forum. The example of the saints and of other living members of the community becomes a powerful form of teaching. Formal and informal ways of instruction are both necessary. Thus, all the faithful have the right to receive instruction in moral teaching in the Church which is faithful both to the gospel and to the signs of the times. At the same time, all the faithful by reasons of their baptism and in light of their different offices, gifts, and talents, have the duty to participate in the moral teaching functions in the Church.

The most characteristic aspect of moral teaching in Roman Catholicism is the hierarchical teaching office. Here the holders of these offices have the duty to exercise their function properly under the gospel, whereas all in the Church have the right to the proper functioning of these offices. Three important aspects of the hierarchical teaching office must be kept in mind.

First, the hierarchical teaching office is not absolute but is subordinate to other important realities. The Constitution on Divine Revelation of Vatican II (n. 10) maintains that "the teaching office is not above the word of God, but serves it." Catholic moral theology in the tradition of Thomas Aquinas has always insisted on an intrinsic morality. Something is commanded because it is good and not the other way around. The hierarchical magisterium must conform itself to what is true and good in moral matters.

Second, the hierarchical magisterium must make every effort to discern the Spirit and the truth properly and must be open to hearing from the experience of all within the Church and even outside it. The process used by the United States bishops in their pastoral letters on peace and the economy well illustrates a proper, wide-ranging process of discernment and consultation.

Third, the hierarchical teaching office must recognize its own limits. It is generally acknowledged that specific moral teaching belongs to the authoritative non-infallible teaching function. Such teachings, in the words of the German bishops, are "by their very nature provisional and entail the possibility of error." Thus there exists at times the possibility and even the right of Catholic believers to dissent from some non-infallible hierarchical teaching.

Discussion Questions

1. From your own experience, what are the most significant ways in which you have received instruction in the Catholic tradition and the presentation of moral teaching in a way that promotes the helpfulness and relevance of Christian values to contemporary life?

2. How would you describe your own duties concerning the obligation to present moral teaching to others in the Catholic community and to society at large?

3. What do you do if you do disagree with a non-infallible hierarchical teaching on a moral issue?

Bibliography

Charles E. Curran and Richard A. McCormick, eds., READINGS IN MORAL THEOLOGY, NUMBER 3: THE MAGISTERIUM AND MORALITY. New York: Paulist Press, 1982.

Francis A. Sullivan, MAGISTERIUM: TEACHING AUTHORITY IN THE CATHOLIC CHURCH. New York: Paulist Press, 1983.

12b. Worship

Kathleen Cannon, OP

All Catholics have the right to receive from the Church those ministries which are needed for the living of a fully Christian life, including:

(b) Worship which reflects the joys and concerns of the gathered community and instructs and inspires it.

The Spirit is very God dwelling within us as our spirit, when, as in St. Paul's phrase, S/He "lays fast hold upon us." It is the Spirit who inaugurates our experiences of grace, enabling us to believe and also answering the summons within us. "The Spirit, too, helps us in our weakness, for we do not know how to pray as we ought; but the Spirit makes intercession for us with groanings that cannot be expressed in speech. He who searches the heart knows what the Spirit means, for the Spirit intercedes for the saints as God himself wills" (Rom. 8:26-27). This is what empowers or enables the Christian to worship. To worship then is more grace or gift that is given to us by God in the Spirit than it is a right to which one lays claim legally or canonically.

It is a question of emphasizing the Church as the holy people of God or the community of the saved as over against the Church as institution, as hierarchical Church. At the same time we cannot have the Church as the community of the saved without some type of structure. That is

---

Kathleen Cannon, OP, is Associate Professor of Communications and Homiletics at the Catholic Theological Union, Chicago IL.

usually explained christologically as the prolongation of Christ in the world. Here it is more fruitful to approach it as the holy people of God or the community of the saved, because this more clearly expresses the pneumatological aspect of the Church; i.e., the Church as being founded by the experience of the Spirit.

The Church lives by the presence of the Spirit in her midst, which is the Spirit once again of the Father and the Son, which means also the Son crucified and the Son raised—and all of those realities are given over to the Christian.

What the Spirit does really is to endow the Christian with freedom, not in the sense of being able to choose as a course of action a or b or c. but freedom in the sense of spontaneity to respond to the love of God offered in Christ and the Spirit. That is what frees us to worship in creative ways.

That is why there is always the historical mediation of God's offer of salvation. The Spirit inspires the Christians of different epochs in different ways depending on particular historical structures. The Spirit is mediated in and through and by way of the different cultural changes that occur in history also. In other words, there is an historical mediation of salvation. So the structures that convey revelation are not purely charismatic.

It is the domain of tradition to insure faithfulness to God's revelation, but what is important is that there is fidelity to a living tradition—and the Spirit is the animator of that. This means there will be a certain provisionary character to the structures the Church uses to celebrate its living faith. Structures cannot be set aside arbitrarily or at will, but there is a certain creativity involved. We are talking about the *free* offer of salvation on the part of God and the *free* acceptance of it on the part of the believer. The revelatory act involves both of those: God's speaking and someone's hearing and listening and responding. Revelation is not simply God making enunciations without these being laid hold of and implemented and interpreted and lived out by the faithful. Tradition is always an interpretive act. One interprets the tradition as one lays hold of it. Our method of interpretation will always begin by asking: What is our situation now? What call is God making precisely in and through our human experience and our experience of the Church? Fidelity to a living tradition then will be found not in doing today what has always been done in the past but rather in responding in new and creative ways to God's offer of salvation in our own historical moment.

All traditions have elements of distortion, and so structures can alienate where they were once meant to unite, can subvert where once they were meant to illuminate. So there has to be a corrective process involved. We speak of "ecclesia semper reformanda,"—the Church always reforming herself because structures can be overstressed or distorted. There is a creativity involved in responding to tradition, but creativity under the impulse or prompting of the Spirit. In other words it is not a purely humanistic occurrence.

All of this is to say that it is the very experience of the Spirit in the Church that makes us restless with the tradition and stirs us to recognize that if worship does not intersect in a meaningful way with peoples' real experience, reflecting their joys and concerns, it is not real but mythological. Furthermore, it is not revelation.

Discussion Questions

1. Does John Courtney Murray's informal definition of worship, "Coming into the Presence," relate to Kathleen Cannon's idea of worship?

2. What are some "creative ways" of worshipping that you have experienced?

3. Do you feel "restless with the tradition"? If so, how does this restlessness manifest itself?

Bibliography

WORSHIP. Published bi-monthly at Collegeville, Minnesota.

D. C. Smolanski, SJ, HOW NOT TO SAY MASS. Paulist Press, Ramsey, New Jersey.

Aidan Kavanaugh, ELEMENTS OF RITE. New York: Pueblo.

12c. Pastoral Counseling

Paul Surlis

All Catholics have the right to receive from the Church those ministries which are needed for the living of a fully Christian life, including: (c) Pastoral counseling that applies with love and effectiveness the Christian heritage to persons in particular situations. (C. 213, C. 217)

Pastoral counseling that applies with love and effectiveness the Christian heritage to persons in particular situations is a right that pertains to the "ministry of alleviation for the 'ailing' among the faithful" of which the Second Vatican Council speaks (*Lumen Gentium* § 28). This ministry is related to but distinct from the ministry of reconciliation which revolves around preaching the word and administering the sacraments (*Lumen Gentium* § 37). Constitutive, also, of the preaching of the gospel is "action on behalf of justice and participation in the transformation of the world" since the Church's mission is "for the redemption of the human race and its liberation from every oppressive situation" (Synod of Bishops: "Justice in the World," 1971, § 6). The ministry of alleviation in one of its specifications pertains to pastoral counseling but this (usually) personal procedure must be performed in full awareness of the socio-political dimensions both of the Gospel and-frequently-of psychic wounds, stress and behavioral disorders.

Paul Surlis is a priest of the diocese of Achonry, Ireland, and teaches Moral Theology and Social Ethics at St. John's University, Jamaica, NY.

82 A Catholic Bill of Rights

The right to assistance from the spiritual heritage of the Church is affirmed for *all* Christians, including pastors, and it is a right inhering in the baptized; it is not a privilege granted by authorities, (*Lumen Gentium* § 37). The obligation to provide trained personnel to enable the fulfillment of the right devolves on pastors whose responsibility it would be to fulfill the conditions necessary for the exercise of the right among all who need pastoral counseling. It must be stressed that persons ordained and lay who engage in pastoral counseling need rigorous training in psycho-therapeutic disciplines together with in-depth formation in the moral, doctrinal and spiritual heritage of Christianity. True pastoral counseling will proceed from "scientific" and religious perspectives and it will be done from a politically aware consciousness. Since this latter dimension is sometimes neglected, it is necessary to draw particular attention to it lest pastoral counseling ally itself with naive psycho-therapeutic techniques which treat stress, anxiety and behavioral problems (personal and familial) in isolation from the social and institutional oppressions which help to generate many (if not most) of them in the first place. One of the greatest temptations for all counselors is to forget that psychic phenomena are not self-generated. They do not spring up unbidden in the psyche. Rather, they also have social, political and economic roots. Furthermore, counseling whether in theory or in practice, that attempts to be purely existential, personal and psychological is not as apolitical as at first it may appear. On the contrary, in attributing anxiety, psychic wounds, behavioral problems to purely personal or inter-personal dynamics it ignores the social contribution to these problems. When the social context (poverty, racism, unemployment, prejudice) is ignored then unjust social institutions go uncriticized and a type of counseling is sanctioned that ultimately is little more than a form of blaming the victim in new guise.

Much contemporary empirical research indicates that e.g., when unemployment increases there is a co-related increase in child abuse, wife-abuse, alcohol-abuse, chemical dependency, anxiety, depression, admission to mental institutions, homicide and suicide. Ulcers, heart-disease and other stress-related illnesses appear to be related to economic conditions even for relatively affluent persons. McNeill speaks of "the great discrepancy between the outer trappings of power and authority and the inner experience of powerlessness that has driven many 'successful' professional people into deep depression and suicide" (McNeill, p. 46).

Anxiety, stress, behavioral problems or marital discord are no less severe for the persons involved because they arise out of, or are exacerbated by, poverty, institutionalized racism, sexism, or other structural oppressions. However, when the structural component is correctly recognized, alleviation of pseudo-guilt may be achieved and attitudes of low self-esteem and self-hatred may be more easily addressed by counselor and client. Gregory Baum, advocating a "politically responsible therapeutic process," makes an important distinction between "one's personal problems" and "one's opposition to the unjust social order." Baum calls this "the therapeutic distinction" and he demonstrates its importance so that persons will not succumb to the temptation of *identifying* their personal problems with the contradictions detected in the social environment. Self-discovery and social struggle are correlative; passion for social transformation cannot substitute for personal healing and growth which, however, in turn is greatly enhanced by involvement in what Baum calls "social praxis" (Baum, p. 101).

Effective preaching can be an important ally of pastoral counseling if it includes a sensitive and courageous exploration of topics such as racial prejudice, sexism, systemic injustice (poverty, bad housing, hunger, homelessness, illiteracy, militarism) in light of the gospel. Moreover, pastoral ministry overall should demonstrate a preferential option for the powerless and marginalized—battered women and children, homophiles, the handicapped, the aged, the divorced, former prisoners, relatives of the imprisoned, victims of crime, the unemployed. Self-help groups modelled on Alcoholics Anonymous should be fostered to facilitate group-therapy in awareness of relevant psychological, religious and social factors. Permission from superiors is not, of course, required to initiate any of these groups but collaboration in their formation between pastoral ministers and those involved is important. Important also is the provision of parish facilities, including the church, for use by each and all of these groups. In this way a parish becomes a network of associations, involved in prayer, solidarity, healing, consciousness-raising and in the struggle for human rights and against all forms of prejudice and discrimination.

The integrity of preaching the gospel of the Reign calls for pastoral counseling that attends to personal and social transformation; one without the other is a distortion, and a failure to apply the Christian heritage to persons in distress, with love and effectiveness.

Discussion Questions

1. In the area in which your local church is situated, are there socio-political conditions that would give rise, among the people of God, to problems requiring pastoral counseling?

2. How could your local Church improve the service of pastoral counseling it provides?

3. Is the preaching in your local Church "an ally of pastoral counseling"? If not, what could be done to help make it so?

Bibliography

Russell Jacoby, SOCIAL AMNESIA: A CRITIQUE OF CONTEMPORARY PSYCHOLOGY FROM ADLER TO LAING. Boston: Beacon Press, 1975.

Juan Luis Segundo, THE HIDDEN MOTIVES OF PASTORAL ACTION: LATIN AMERICAN REFLECTIONS. Maryknoll, NY: Orbis Books, 1972.

James A. Coriden, Thomas J. Green, Donald E. Heintschel, eds., THE CODE OF CANON LAW A TEXT AND COMMENTARY, commissioned by the Canon Law Society of America, see especially canons 213, 215 and commentary pp. 147, 149. New York: Paulist Press, 1984.

Gregory Baum, "The Retrieval of Subjectivity," CANADIAN JOURNAL OF COMMUNITY MENTAL HEALTH, Vol. No. 1, March, 1982, pp. 89-102.

John McNeill, S.J., "Spiritual Values in Therapy: A Theological Perspective," THE BULLETIN OF THE NATIONAL GUILD OF CATHOLIC PSYCHIATRISTS, Vol. 26, 1980, pp. 37-51.

13. Authentic Self-Realization

Margaret Brennan, IHM

All Catholics have the right, while being mindful of Gospel norms, to follow whatever paths will enhance their life in Christ (i.e., their self-realization as unique human beings created by God). They also have the right to guidance that will foster authentic human living both on a personal level and in relation to their communities and the world. (C.213)

Authentic self-realization as a Christian right is deeply rooted in both the Hebrew Scriptures and the writings of the New Testament. In our own times it has received renewed emphasis in a number of Church documents as well as in the writings of popes, and bishops from all around the world. This has been particularly evident in those statements which reiterate the call for the fullest development of all that is human in personal and family life as well as in the political and economic structures and institutions within which human persons live and work. In our own century, the contributions of the behavioral sciences have opened new vistas in the journey of human development and, as a result, have modified certain aspects in the Church's traditional ascetical teaching and widened the parameters of both pastoral counseling

---

Margaret Brennan, IHM, is Professor of Pastoral Theology at Regis College in the Toronto School of Theology, Toronto, Canada.

and of spiritual direction. Unfortunately, much of the ascetical teaching of the Church has regarded self-realization as disordered self-love in need of curbing, and has not equally stressed the deeper disorder of self-hatred which prevents human beings from reaching their full potential to grow in the likeness of Jesus Christ in a community of fellowship and faith. The scriptures, particularly the New Testament, give us a much more balanced view and point out how Christians can be a source of enlightenment and growth to one another in their journey toward true self-realization.

The meaning of this right, as is true of so many others, cannot be adequately understood by itself. Self-realization and continued human becoming, if it is to avoid the narrow constraints of self-centeredness, must be seen in the context of a wider corporate responsibility which is also mutually conditioned and includes the Christian imperative of on-going conversion. Authentic self-realization in the covenant community of Israel and in the Christian People of God is a right that does not stand alone, as the Scriptures point out. Moreover, coming to true self-realization and to corporate responsibility is achieved through truthful and loving dialogue. It is through this dialogue that human beings come to that self-knowledge by which we experience ourselves as still in the process of growth and development. In a very real sense this is the meaning of spiritual direction.

In the Johannine Gospel, Jesus declares that he has come that we "...may have life, and have it more fully" (Jn. 10:10). These words hearken back to the words of God's covenant with the Israelites as spoken through Moses: "Choose life, that you and your descendants may live" (Dt. 30:19). Here is an invitation to enter into the essential meaning of self-realization. The Lucan Gospel, which stresses the universality of salvation, nuances the call to self-realization, without demanding that all walk the same way, as is seen in the pericope of Martha and Mary (Lk. 10:38-42). Moreover, in this same gospel, Jesus' respect for persons, and the invitation to true human becoming which calls for conversion, is manifest in the forgiveness offered to the woman who was a sinner (Lk. 7:36-50) and to Zacchaeus the senior tax collector "Today salvation has come to this house, because this man too is a son of Abraham" (Lk. 19:9).

The letter of Paul to the Romans underscores the call of Jesus to true freedom and therefore to authentic self-realization. "The reasons, therefore, why those who are in Christ Jesus are not condemned is that the law of the spirit of life in Christ Jesus has set you free from the law of sin and death" (Rom. 8:1). The theme is repeated in Galatians, when Paul writes, "When Christ freed us, he meant us to remain free" (Gal. 5:1). That such true self-realization is not an invitation to self-indulgence is manifestly clear in verses 13-25. Here we are counseled to test the "spirit" of our freedom and to recognize its source. "Since the Spirit is our life, let us be directed by the Spirit" (Gal. 5:26).

The right to self-realization and to the guidance that fosters authentic human living is repeated in the mystical tradition of the Church. A reading of the *Life* of Teresa of Avila graphically illustrates this right in terms of the call to contemplative prayer. Indeed, it is the basis of her reform.

In modern times, the theme of self-realization becomes a kind of motif running through almost all Church documents and exhortations. They speak of the dehumanizing tendencies and structures of modern culture which militate against the ability of the human spirit "to wonder, to understand, to contemplate, to make personal judgments, and to develop a religious, moral, and social sense" (*Gaudium et Spes*, No. 59). Paul VI points out that "human fulfillment constitutes, as it were, a summary of our duties" (*Populorum Progressio*, no. 16) and that this fulfillment is communal as well as personal. "It is not just certain individuals, but all persons who are called to this fullness of development" (no. 17). John Paul II has repeated this right in almost every country and culture of the world.

Discussion Questions

1. How do we deal creatively with the tension between the rights of the individual and the responsibility to the community?

2. What concrete practices and attitudes enhance this tension between the individuality of each person and the totality of the community?

3. How can we better develop both individual and communal forms of spiritual direction that can promote the right of the individual to self-realization within the reality of human solidarity?

Bibliography

Teresa of Avila, THE COLLECTED WORKS OF ST. TERESA OF AVILA, Vol. I, "The Book of Her Life." Translated by Kieran Kavanaugh, O.C.D. and Otilio Rodriguez, O.C.D.: Washington: ICS Publications, Institute of Carmelite Studies.

William A. Barry and William J. Connolly, THE PRACTICE OF SPIRITUAL DIRECTION. New York: Seabury Press, 1982.

Karl Rahner, "The Spirituality of the Church of the Future," THEOLOGICAL IN-VESTIGATIONS, Vol. 20. New York: Crossroads, 1981.

14. Custom and Laws of the Rite

Archimandrite Victor J. Pospishil

All Catholics have the right to follow the customs and laws of the rite of their choice and to worship accordingly. (C.214)

The right of Catholics to worship God according to their ritual and the spiritual traditions of their own ecclesial heritage (C. 214) was, till Vatican II, understood as chiefly referring to forms of worship. While the difference of liturgical rites referred primarily to the various Eastern Churches, (C. 214) would include also the few local remnants of Latin rites other than the Roman rite, such as the Ambrosian rite in northern Italy and the Mozarabic rite in Spain. As to the Eastern Churches, the understanding of the right of Catholics to follow their own ecclesial heritage was extended to include the matrix of the liturgical and spiritual differences, the separate corporate existence of these autonomous associated churches of the Catholic Church.

It is now established that every Catholic belongs in the first place to one of the ritual Churches, and only through membership in one's own Church is one a member of the Universal Catholic Church (C. 111, 112), headed by the Bishop of Rome, the successor of St. Peter (C. 331). The

---

Victor J. Pospishil is Vicar Judicial of the diocese of Stanford, CT.

pope presides over this communion of Churches, Latin and Eastern. Each of these Churches is a Christian community in its own right (*ecclesia sui iuris*), comprised of a hierarchy and faithful. One of them, and in numbers of faithful by far the largest today, is the Latin Church, the head of which is the pope in his capacity of Patriarch of the West. The other ritual churches are today all of an Eastern ritual tradition, more than twenty, but there is the possibility that also other Western ritual Churches could be created, such as the discussed possibility of a reunion between the Universal Catholic Church of Rome and the Anglican Church.

This new recognition of the true ecclesial character of the various Eastern Catholic communities has relegated the term "Rite" to the realm of liturgical forms of worship, and is in other aspects expressed by the term "Church."

From the right to preserve one's ritual-spiritual heritage within one's own ritual Church there follow other rights, such as for each Church to have a hierarchy of its own. The Eastern Catholic churches are distinguished among themselves by being headed by hierarchs with the dignity of patriarch (Coptic Patriarchate of Alexandria, Melkite P. of Antioch, Maronite P. of Antioch, Syrian P. of Antioch, Armenian P., Chaldean P.), major archbishops of patriarchal rank (Ukrainian Church), and other churches headed by metropolitans or by bishops (Romanian, Ruthenian, Malabarian, Malankarian, Ethiopian Metropolias; Hungarian Byzantine, Italo-Albanian, Slovak Byzantine eparchies). The hierarchical structures of various Eastern Catholic churches will have to be revised after the Eastern Catholic Code of Canon Law is promulgated, perhaps as early as in 1988.

From the character of being a Church in its own right each Catholic ritual Church derives the authority to have its own system of law. Each Eastern Catholic Church shares basic legal principles with the Latin ritual Church as well as with the other Eastern Catholic Churches. Thus, it was possible to initiate a codification of the laws of these Churches not for each Church separately, a procedure which would have been too cumbersome and impractical, but to prepare one code of canon law for all the Eastern Catholic Churches, which will contain the norms that are common to all. Each of these Churches will in addition prepare its own particular law.

For members of any ritual Church it is important to be entitled to continue the forms of worship as handed down from the ancestors, usually going back to apostolic times. This includes the possibility of following one's own calendar (Gregorian vs. Julian; *OE* 20); rules of fast or abstinence in respect to times and forms; administration of the sacraments according to their own laws, as, e.g., when the priest confers chrismation (confirmation) at once with baptism (C.842 #2), or when infants receive the eucharist with baptism. The once apparent differences between the liturgy of the Latin Church and those of the various Eastern Churches have been very much reduced by the liturgical reform in the Latin Church in the wake of Vatican II, which consisted often in a return to the forms of the ancient Church, still preserved in the Eastern Churches.

Catholics are permitted to frequent the divine services in any Catholic rite other than their own (*OE* 21, c.1248,1) and to receive the sacraments of penance (*OE* 16, c.991) and eucharist not only on special occasions but permanently on a regular basis (*OE* 13,14); c.842 2). If they are living away from a church of their own ritual tradition, they are placed under the care of the local Catholic pastor of another rite, and if no diocese of theirs is established there, they come under the authority of the local Catholic bishop of another church, usually of the Latin Church. If their number warrants it, the bishop must establish for them parishes of their ritual tradition, and appoint perhaps even a separate episcopal vicar and dean (CC.383 2; 475; 518; 553). When the number of such communities increases, the Holy See will see to it that a bishop of their own is appointed for them. Thus, in the United States and in Canada there are ecclesiastical provinces and dioceses for the faithful of the Armenian, Chaldean, Maronite, Melkite, Romanian, Ruthenian, Slovak, Ukrainian Churches, and others are being contemplated.

The rite of the Latin Church being represented in all countries of the world, the protection of the rights of Catholics to worship in accordance with their own heritage refers practically to Catholics of the Eastern churches. It may sometimes become applicable also to Latin Catholics when it is a question of difference of language and ethnic and cultural aspects (C. 518).

The Eastern Churches have always been convinced that a Christian is entitled to participate on Sundays in the communal eucharistic sacrifice. The substitution of the divine liturgy by some prayer service, liturgy of the word, even with distribution of holy communion by a non-priest, was not considered adequate. Consequently, they have ordained a sufficient number of priests even if they were married men and possessed only a rudimentary professional education, although giving preference to celibate candidates, and making the unmarried status a requisite for bishops. The prohibition of the Holy See against ordaining married candidates to the priesthood outside the original regions of the respective Eastern Catholic Churches, as in the USA and Canada, has never been observed fully, and will be abrogated with the promulgation of the new Eastern Catholic Code of Canon Law.

The attendance at Sunday and holyday liturgy, while still obligatory in a general way for all Catholics, is today positively viewed as an opportunity and a right vis-a-vis the Church. In the event of the unavailability of a Sunday Mass in one's own rite, a Catholic is not obliged to attend it in another. But all Catholics are permitted to attend the divine services of the Eastern non-Catholics and receive the sacraments from their priests, especially in case of necessity (*OE*, c.844, 3).

Discussion Questions

1. What would be the advantages/disadvantages of the Roman Catholic rite's returning to the custom of conferring Confirmation on infants at Baptism and of giving the infants the Eucharist at the same time?

2. Are there any non-Roman-rite communities in your vicinity? If so, is there any attempt by either rite's adherents to get to know the other rite's tradition?

Bibliography

OE = ORIENTALIUM ECCLESIARUM, the Decree on the Eastern Catholic Churches of Vatican II.

James Coriden, Thomas J. Green, Donald E. Heintschel, eds., CANON LAW SOCIETY OF AMERICA COMMENTARY: THE CODE OF CANON LAW. A TEXT AND COMMENTARY. New York: Paulist Press, 1985, pp. 23, 78, 121, 268.

Victor J. Pospishil and John D. Faris, NEW LATIN CODE OF CANON LAW AND EASTERN CATHOLICS. Brooklyn: Diocese of St. Maron, 1984.

15. Sacraments

Robert Nugent, SDS

All Catholics, regardless of race, age, nationality, sex, sexual orientation, state-of-life, or social position have the right to receive all the sacraments for which they are adequately prepared. (C. 213, C. 843:1)

The first right for lay persons mentioned in the Conciliar document *Lumen Gentium* (37) is the right to the "spiritual goods" of the Church, especially the Word of God and the sacraments. This fundamental right is rooted in Christian baptism. It is not a privilege given to the laity by ecclesiastical authorities. The new Code of Canon Law (C. 213) speaks of this right as belonging to "the Christian Faithful" and not only to Catholics. Theoretically, the Code recognizes the right of non-Catholic Christians as baptized members of the Church to receive the sacraments. Access to penance, the sacrament of the sick and, especially, the Eucharist, however, is restricted by various Church regulations. Article 15 of the Charter of the Association for the Right of Catholics in the Church promotes this right for Catholics regardless of certain personal characteristics. This essay will concern itself with certain groups of Catholics whose rights in this area may seem to be threatened by exclusion from certain sacraments.

Robert Nugent, SDS, is Co-Founder of New Ways Ministry and lecturer and writer in ministry to homosexual people

The right to the sacraments is so basic in the life of the Church that bishops can develop various means to facilitate the exercise of that right. This might include authorizing deacons and lay persons to baptize and to witness marriages. It could also be argued that the right to the sacraments, especially the Eucharist, is so crucial to the spiritual well-being of the community that in the absence or critical shortage of ordained ministers to preside at the Eucharist, Church authorities could make provision for the ordination of married men, and the reinstatement of resigned priests. The ordination of women, while a separate theological issue, surely has some critical pastoral implications.

The ARCC Charter (15) declaration that "all Catholics" regardless of "sex" have the right to receive "all the sacraments" for which they are adequately prepared is implicit support for the ordination of qualified women. While it is argued that no one strictly speaking has a personal or legal "right" to ordination, many argue for a right to have one's qualifications and call tested by the community's leaders and representatives. Right 16 is further support for women's ordination to a renewed priestly ministry when it promotes the right for all Catholics to exercise "all ministries" in the Church for which they are "adequately prepared." Those who oppose such ordination and ministry because women lack a certain physical resemblance to the physical Jesus might logically have to argue that due to a lack of physical requirements, women are not adequately prepared!

Along with "sex" in relation to the sacrament of orders, two other characteristics listed in right 15 of ARCC's Charter require additional comment. These are "sexual orientation" and "state of life" as they apply to particular sacraments. Two groups of Catholics—active homosexuals and those in "irregular" or invalid marriages which are beyond canonical regularizing in the external forum of the Church's marriage tribunal—are, at least in popular Catholic opinion, excluded from the sacraments, especially the Eucharist, because of a lack of adequate preparation, namely, their being in the "state of grace" or free from serious sin. For some reason there is less concern about racist individuals, tax cheats, corrupt politicians or Catholic heads of repressive governments.

Does a Catholic have a "right" to the sacrament of marriage regardless of sexual orientation? The Church does recognize the right of a homosexual individual to enter a sacramental heterosexual marriage, provided the person can engage in the physical act of heterosexual intercourse. This is in keeping with a concept of marriage more along legal contractual lines involving the exchange of exclusive rights to inter-course. If a developing theology of marriage views the relationship more as a communion of persons with the concomitant emotional and spiritual reciprocity, however, then the right of a true homosexual per-son can be restricted for the good of the individual and the community. The trend of marriage tribunals to annul marriages involving constitu-tional homosexual individuals because of "psychic incapacity," seems to confirm the wisdom of restricting the right in certain cases due to lack of adequate preparation.

Theoretically, the right of a homosexual male to apply and prepare for ordination is not at issue. Historically, bishops have always—know-ingly or not—ordained homosexual persons to the priesthood and epis-copacy. For both homosexual and heterosexual candidates a genuine willingness and proven ability to embrace a celibate commitment as re-quired in current Church discipline are part of being adequately prepared. An exception to this was the decision of the Catholic bishops of Massachusetts to deny the right to ordination for the priesthood to homosexual candidates. The bishops wrote that only those who had reached "heterosexual maturity" should be accepted for priesthood.

One further restriction is often placed on homosexual candidates for the priesthood and priests themselves and that is that they keep their sexual orientation out of the public eye. Even here some case might be mounted for the right of an openly homosexual and celibate individual to be accepted provided he is otherwise adequately prepared, since magisterial teaching terms the homosexual orientation "morally neu-tral." A pastoral plan from the archdiocese of San Francisco goes even further and says that homosexuality can be a "building block" in the search for unity and harmony. The archdiocese of Baltimore calls the homosexual orientation a "starting point for one's response to Christ's call to perfection."

The other sacrament which relates directly both to "sexual orienta-tion" and "state of life" is the Eucharist. Canon 843.1 supports the right of Christians to the sacraments as grounded in Canon 213. Sacred mini-sters are obliged not to deny the sacraments to those who are "properly disposed" and who are "not prohibited from receiving them." Canon 912 further stipulates that any baptized persons who are not prohibited by law must be admitted to Holy Communion because of his/her right to this sacrament in accord with Canon 213. The questions which arise in this connection concern homosexual people in a stable, committed relationship characterized by homogenital expression, and Catholics in invalid marriages. Do these Catholics have any right to the Eucharist? Are they properly disposed? Can and should the minister who knows of these situations deny them Holy Communion?

Although Canon Law protects the right of the baptized to Holy Communion it also applies some restrictions on certain groups such as non-Catholic Christians, children, the mentally handicapped and "grave sinners." Canon 915, for example, says that those who "obstinately persist in manifest grave sin are not to be admitted to Holy Communion." Reputable commentators define a "manifest" sin as one which is publicly known even if only by a few; "obstinate persistence" means that a person persists in the sin or sinful situation and does not heed the warnings of Church authorities or adhere to Church teachings. Can the right of Catholics to the sacrament of the Eucharist be circumscribed by requirements such as good faith, complete adherence to Church doctrines and the absence of what is called objectively grave sin which might bar people from Communion?

Two approaches seem possible. The first arises from current Church practice, which says that a minister cannot simply assume that in the internal forum of personal conscience either homogenital expression or sexual expression in a canonically irregular marriage is necessarily gravely sinful. Any doubt about either the gravity of the sin or the public nature of the situation is to be resolved in favor of the person who approaches the Lord's table. The question of doubt is a key issue if we are to avoid both a disrespect for the Eucharist and treating Communion as a form of "cheap grace."

The theologian authors of *Human Sexuality* defined both the need for and the right to the sacraments for homosexual as well as heterosexual Christians. In determining whether or not to administer Holy Communion a pastor can be guided by the general principle of Catholic moral theology that only a morally certain obligation can be imposed. Thus, the obligation not to admit certain active homosexual people and others to the Eucharist must be based on the certainty of the gravity of the sin or on its public nature. An unresolvable doubt of either the law or the fact allows one to follow a true and solidly probable opinion in favor of the liberty to receive and administer Holy Communion. The same authors hold that in the light of already "existing doubts" and un-answered questions about homosexuality, including the possibility of evaluating some homosexual expression as other than "intrinsically evil," a solidly probable opinion can be invoked in favor of permitting some active homosexual Catholics freedom of conscience and free access to full Eucharistic fellowship.

Although *Human Sexuality* was not well received by certain Church authorities it did find some support in other quarters. The Roman Catholic bishops of England and Wales, for example, quoted *Human Sexuality* almost verbatim in their discussion on a solidly probable opin-ion permitting reception of the Eucharist by homosexual Catholics. Likewise, the archdiocese of San Francisco quoted the same advice on the same issue but identified the source as the British document, *An Introduction To The Pastoral Care Of Homosexual People.* The San Fran-cisco document also noted that the two elements which clearly exclude Christians from the Eucharist are lack of personal faith and the commit-ment to or awareness of personal, serious sin. Given the fact that the context of the section quoted by the English bishops and repeated in the San Francisco document concerning serious doubt about the fact of the intrinsic evil of all homosexual expression, the right of some homosexual Catholics to receive Communion seems to be established on rather solid theological, pastoral and canonical grounds. As the authors conclude: "All else being equal, a homosexual engaging in homosexual acts in good conscience has the same right of conscience and the same rights to the sacraments as a married couple practicing birth control in good con-science."

Similar reasoning was employed by Archbishop John Quinn speaking as President of the National Conference of Catholic bishops at the 1980 World Synod of bishops in Rome. Quinn told the Synod delegates that many American Catholics regularly receive the Eucharist while refusing to conform to the papal teaching on birth control in *Humanae Vitae.* He indicated that he considered their Communions to be in good faith and said that they could not be charged with "obduracy, ignorance or bad will." According to one commentator, "he evidenced no inclination to regard their noncompliance with authentic Catholic teaching as grounds for discouraging them from frequenting the Eucharist."

In the same year, writing of homosexuality, however, the archbishop said that in order to receive the Eucharist one must be "living in harmony with the moral and doctrinal teaching of the Church" and that homosexual persons who wish to receive Communion "must be honestly following the moral teaching of the Church or at least sincerely striving to live up to that teaching."

For Catholics in invalid marriages the right to receive Holy Communion regardless of their "state of life" was clearly articulated in responses that came from Rome concerning the internal forum or the sacrament of reconciliation. Responses in 1973 and 1975 said "Those couples may be allowed to receive the sacraments on two conditions, that they try to live according to the demands of Christian moral principles and that they receive the sacraments in churches in which they are not known so that they will not create any scandal."

A second approach to the right of active homosexual people, the invalidly married and others to receive Holy Communion regardless of their "state of life," involves an ecclesiology and theology of Eucharist and Communion in the Christian community. If perfect doctrinal unity and conformity both in thought and behavior with Church teachings is a prerequisite for Communion, then Communion is perceived as a reward for being worthy. But the Church can be seen as a fellowship of believing people in constant need of mercy, as a community of personal acceptance and support offering divine healing. Then the Eucharist is not seen as a reward for the pure or the perfect. Catholic faith already sees the spiritual support and nourishment of the Eucharist as the foremost source of grace to meet a need for personal and communal health, for ecclesial unity and for forgiveness, and as food for pilgrim people on the way to the reign of God.

There is an analogy to be drawn here between certain nonconforming Catholics and non-Catholic Christians who are at times admitted to the Eucharist. Church authorities discourage indiscriminate intercommunion because full Eucharistic communion presupposes, signifies and strengthens full ecclesial communion—something which does not yet exist. But once some common agreements are reached on central issues such as baptism, the nature and mission of the Church, ordained ministry and Eucharist, then gradual and supervised table-sharing at the Eucharist can promote even further agreement on other less central issues including the type, style and exercise of gospel authority. Vatican II's declaration on ecumenism taught that the basic premise on which participation in the Eucharist by non-Catholic Christians can be legitimated is the unity of the Church and the sharing in the means of grace. It can be sometimes desirable to make eucharistic grace available to non-Catholic Christians who are in good faith despite the absence of their full incorporation into the Church's faith and government. Surely it can be no less desirable for eucharistic grace to be shared by Catholic believers who are in good faith despite their intellectual and/or behavioral nonconformity to certain of the Church's teachings about homosexuality, contraception and second marriages.

Discussion Questions

1. If the community does not maintain certain clear standards and conditions for fruitful reception of the Eucharist, is there not some serious and real danger that Communion can be treated simply as a social or cultural ritual with little or no personal, spiritual or theological meaning?

2. Is the internal forum or "conscience solution" for homosexual and remarried Catholics an adequate pastoral solution or does it still make such Catholics second-class members of the Church?

3. Have you personally ever felt yourself excluded for any reason from any of the sacraments and, if so, for what reasons, and how did you respond to the situation and feelings provoked?

Bibliography

NOT SERVANTS BUT FRIENDS, Reflections on Human Rights in the and Freedom in the Church, Barbara Cullom and Richard Dieter, eds. Quixote Center, Box 5206, Hyattsville, Maryland 20782.

B. Williams, "Gay Catholics and Eucharistic Communion," R. Nugent ed., A CHALLENGE TO LOVE: GAY AND LESBIAN CATHOLICS IN THE CHURCH. New York: Crossroad, 1983.

L. Boff, CHURCH, CHARISM AND POWER. New York: Crossroad, 1985, especially the chapter titled "The Violations of Human Rights in the Church."

16. Exercise of Ministries

William R. Burrows

*All Catholics, regardless of canonical status (lay or clerical), sex
or sexual orientation, have the right to exercise all ministries in the
Church for which they are adequately prepared, according to the
needs of and with the approval of the community. (C. 225:1, C.
274:1, C. 1024)*

The word "ministry" stems directly from the Latin "*ministrare*" and
the Greek "*diakonein*," and means "to serve." Although not many years
ago it was still thought to be a "Protestant" term, ministry has lately become both more important and frequently used, as the Roman Catholic
Church returns to using it as a central category for delineating what the
church is and does.

To understand what is implied when the ARCC Charter claims that
all Catholics have a right to exercise *all* ministries for which they are
adequately prepared, according to the needs of and with the approval of
the community, involves grasping: (1) the profound ambiguity of serving
in any fashion; (2) the dialogic criterion implied in the rights charter;
and (3) the evangelical criterion of *agape* implied in all ecclesial service.

The ideal image of service is that of dedication to help one's fellows,
to be sure, but the ambiguity of service is revealed if one ponders the un-
examined side of the term. To serve as a cabinet minister is to have a

---

William Burrows is the author of "New Ministries: The Global Context" (Orbis) and works in the education group of the American Medical Association.

powerful, prestigious post in the governance of the commonwealth, and the possibility of serving millions well. To serve at tables is to be far from the top of the socio-economic ladder, but also offers the possibility of serving others well. Both ministries are important, but each has soul-endangering qualities, as an existential analysis of the problem of *ressentiment* reveals. Serving others places the server and the one served in a highly charged relationship. If love and respect for one another are absent, the atmosphere becomes lethal to the party which does not respect the basic humanity of the other.

When one considers Christian service, this danger is doubly present. The minister easily becomes dehumanized in one way; and the one ministered to dehumanized in another, as Nietzsche (who is at this point perhaps Christianity's most important critic) reminds us when he observes that Christianity preaches love, but has perhaps been even more successful in breeding brittle resentments between classes, as it forces them to cloak their hostilities in pious gestures of mutual respect.

To minister effectively at all to others is to exert authority and power, in at least the etymological sense of the word authority (from *"augere,"* to make grow or increase), by assisting another to grow. The art of Christian service is to make the exercise of personal authority or power an exercise of respectful love aligned with divine benevolence to enhance the stature of the one being served. And the dark side of the present Roman Catholic praxis of ministry and authority is that those who officially exercise authority in the name of the Church use ideology to keep office in the hands of members of their own class. Thus they are in the grips of a distortion of reality which they seem unable to unmask.

Those who are barred by the clerical ideology from exercising the gifts they possess and wish to use in the Church or for the world, however, are also in danger, for they can self-indulgently believe that they, simply because they are denied power, have the spirit of service which the New Testament remembers Jesus as having. Gospel life is rather more nuanced than that. Dialogue between the one wishing to offer service and the community whom he or she wishes to serve is a delicate but important aspect of the call to ministry. Without that intersubjective dialogue, Christian service can easily degenerate into moral posturing quite a ways removed from love of the other precisely as a worthy other.

The ARCC Charter, correctly I think, affirms that all Christians have a right to exercise ministries for which they are properly prepared and to which the community calls them. The danger of using the term "right," borrowed from the Anglo-Saxon political terminology of struggling to wrest "rights" from kings who thought they ruled "by divine 'right,'" is: The *dialogic criterion* for entering into ministry (mutual discerning of the presence of God by respectful dialogue between the community and the individual who seeks to serve) could be omitted by those in pursuit of ministries they may wish to exercise in or on behalf of the Church. One does not have to be in favor of the present clerical promotion system to observe that a purely self-selective system can produce some rather inappropriate matches between ministries and prospective ministers.

John's Gospel's Jesus, then, is a wise man when he allows Peter to exert authority in the community only if he loves more genuinely than his fellow disciples (Jn 21:15-20), thus making *agape*, self-forgetting love that regards every human person as being of supreme value, the *evangelical criterion* for ministry. Catholics forget that at their peril. But if they remember it, then, ARCC's 16th article is a significant reminder that no ideology should bar spirit-filled lovers of God, women, men and children from exercising whatever ministries they are suited for.

It is common to hear people speak of ministry in the Church as service. We often hear them say as well that we need to retrieve the synoptic memory of Jesus living as one who "came to serve, not to be served" (Mt. 20:28; Lk. 22:24-27). As laudable as this is, it may also be naive if such calls fail to retrieve and overcome another aspect of Church history: that is to say, in other words, the factors which make it seem plausible to the Roman Catholic hierarchy that only celibate males can exercise ordained ministry in the church today. It is fact, as Berger and Luckmann remind us, that reality—even religious reality, which is supposedly revealed and exists in the church *de jure divino* (by divine right)—is socially and historically constructed. It can thus be deconstructed and reconstructed when history's demands make that process the thing to do, if one is to be responsible to a tradition's deeper dynamism. But until *that* principle is accepted and applied to religious change, there is little likelihood that Church law will change.

Canons 277 and 1024 unambiguously state that, "Clerics . . . are obliged to observe celibacy," and "Only a baptized male validly receives sacred ordination," thus barring the married and women from exercising central roles in ecclesial leadership. In essence, then, the ARCC Charter of Rights raises the question of whether Church law improperly restricts admission to the roles of liturgical leadership, public teaching and ecclesial governance, since access to these ministries is denied to well over half the Church's members.

The 16th article of the ARCC Charter rests on the principle that the liberating message of a passage undoubtedly written by Paul (Galatians 3:27ff, ". . . neither Jew nor Greek . . . neither slave nor free . . . neither male nor female") carries more weight than problematic texts such as 1 Cor 14:34ff ("Women shall keep silence in churches"), or a text from 1 Timothy that had great practical influence in the first several centuries, when the Church was hardening its doctrine on who could be a recognized office-bearer. (1 Tim. 3:2ff states flatly that the church overseer—"*episkopos*"—is to be a man—"*aner*").

The 16th Article of the Charter asks that the Church face squarely, too, the question of where homosexuals fit in ecclesial ministry. The New Testament remains silent on whether a homosexual *orientation* should bar either a male or a female from office, and from that silence very little should be inferred. Indeed, prescinding entirely from the question of the morality of homosexual *activity*, the memory of the New Testament is that Jesus was a man of compassion interested in purity of heart and apt to show anger at those who insisted upon wooden application of the Mosaic law. In the case of people with every other quality for exercising a ministry in the Church, would it not be better for a Church living close to the dangerous memory of its wineskin-bursting teacher to be daring, and say in effect something like the following? "We prefer a homosexual leader who loves God and humankind with homosexual affectivity and orientation over affectless asexuality,—and we want also the right to choose either married or single heterosexually-oriented men or women."

The Roman Catholic hierarchy has little difficulty in recognizing every Catholic's right to carry on the most important ministries, such as caring for the poor and disadvantaged (Mt. 25:31-46), or paying worship to God with one's whole heart, mind and soul (Mt. 22:37). These ministries lie at the center of the Christian ethos. The puzzle is that Church law denies ministries of lesser importance to those who could, in many cultural contexts, exercise them within their communities. It would seem far more reasonable to accept the principle enshrined in the ARCC Charter, and probably also far more conducive to the good health of the community, that it have the right to entrust ministries to anyone it judges capable of exercising them for the community's benefit and in the spirit of the gospel.

Discussion Questions

1. How do you respond to Nietzsche's criticism that Christianity, while preaching love, "breeds brittle resentments between classes"?

2. Is there indeed "a danger in using the term right" in this context?

3. What bearing does this right have on today's "vocation crisis" in the West?

Bibliography

Peter Berger and Thomas Luckmann, THE SOCIAL CONSTRUCTION OF REALITY. Garden City, New York: Doubleday, 1966, furnishes a readable entry-point into the so-called "sociology of knowledge," and deals well with the important topic of how the "plausibility" of an idea (e.g., the ordination of women) is practically more important than any proof of the idea's "truth."

Hans von Campenhausen, ECCLESIASTICAL AUTHORITY AND SPIRITUAL POWER IN THE CHURCH OF THE FIRST THREE CENTURIES. Stanford: Stanford University Press, 1969; German edition, KIRCHLICHES AMT UND GEISTLICHE VOLLMACHT. Tuebingen: J.C.B. Mohr, 1953, gives an excellent account of the broad range of spiritual, religious and social factors that entered into the development of ecclesiastical office.

Elisabeth Schuessler Fiorenza, IN MEMORY OF HER: A FEMINIST THEOLOGICAL RECONSTRUCTION OF CHRISTIAN ORIGINS. New York: Crossroad, 1983, examines in detail the evidence that patriarchal forces, active in both the development of the scriptural canon and ecclesial praxis in regard to women, gradually obscured the original egalitarian character of the Christian community.

Edward Schillebeeckx, "The Catholic Understanding of Office in the Church," THEOLOGICAL STUDIES 30 (1969), pp. 567-87 is a tightly reasoned argument for allowing the forms and structures of ministry to follow local social mores and structures. It can serve also as a precis to the most important arguments of Schilleebeckx's MINISTRY: LEADERSHIP IN THE COMMUNITY OF JESUS CHRIST. New York: Crossroad, 1981, which is perhaps the most important theological work available for situating ministry in the context of integral ecclesial life.

17. Church Office-holders

Anthony T. Padovano

*All Catholics have the right to have Church office-holders foster a
sense of community.* (C. 369, C. 515)

The purpose of the Church is the creation of *communio* or community. This objective is verified vertically when a relationship with
God occurs; it is achieved horizontally when friendship and faith are
shared among believers. In both cases, the function of the office-holder
is neither the preservation of one's own status nor the subordination of
others to one's own sphere of influence. The office-holder is effective in
direct proportion to his/her ability to serve as a means to these larger
purposes.

The New Testament offers abundant evidence for the priority of
community over office-holder. The Synoptics portray the Christian
community as a place where the power structures by which the world is
organized are broken down and eliminated. Matthew states it clearly:

> You know that among the pagans the rulers lord it over them
> and their great men make their authority felt. This is not to
> happen among you. No, anyone who wants to be great among
> you must be your servant (Matt. 20:25-26).

Anthony Padovano is Professor of Literature and Theology at Ram-
apo College, Mahwah, NJ, and Fordham University, New York City.

Mark 10:42 and Luke 22:25 repeat the saying with almost identical words. Office-holders are exhorted, furthermore, never to be "dictators over any group that is put in your charge" (1 Peter 5:3).

John's Gospel shifts the focus from office-holders to the Paraclete or to a personal relationship with Jesus. John's concept of community is vertical, but his stress on love assures that no minister would choose office over community.

New Testament ministry, in general, does not develop around liturgy, Eucharist or authority but around the concept of community. Some of these ministries have more influence than others, but ministry is function rather that state, and community is the center of attention.

The model for all this, of course, is the ministry of Jesus. Jesus calls for solidarity and equality among Christians. He protests when fundamental rights are not respected. The cleansing of the Temple episode is an angry rejection of priestly rulers whose wealth derives from exploitation. This incident seals the fate of Jesus.

In our own day, the Second Vatican Council recaptures these themes. The Church is not a large multi-national organization with diocesan representatives but rather a community of communities, a gathering together of individual Churches which become "The one and only Catholic Church" (*Lumen Gentium*, 23). It is not authority that holds the Church together but collegiality and *communio* .

This dynamic is active also on the diocesan level. A diocese is a "portion of God's People" (*Christus Dominus*, 11). People are to be shepherded, not ruled, and to be formed not by jurisdiction but by the Holy Spirit, the Gospel and the Eucharist. Office-holders are servants and friends, not rulers and masters. God makes Christians holy by "making them into a single people" (*Lumen Gentium*, 9). Indeed, no one is saved, even though "part of the body of the Church," unless that person "perseveres in charity" (*Lumen Gentium*, 14). One hears in this the echo of John's Gospel.

The community which is the Church is not defined primarily as an institution, but as the People of God, the Body of Christ, the Temple of the Spirit (*Lumen Gentium*, 17). An office-holder in such a structure either fosters community or abuses his/her office.

Canon Law brings into the legal code the biblical insights of the New Testament and the theology of Vatican II. It gives official recognition, for the first time in law to the principle of subsidiarity (cf. Principles for Revision, 5). Subsidiarity decentralizes authority and decision-making.

The Revised Code describes the diocese as a community rather than as a subdivision of a larger entity (C. 369). It is a portion of God's People. Territoriality is not constitutive of its nature but merely determinative. It is constituted by faith and sacraments, by community, and by the ministry or service of the bishop.

A parish, furthermore, is not a subdivision of a diocese but "a definite community of the Christian faithful" (C. 515). Territoriality is not dealt with until three canons later (C. 518).

It is clear from every crucial point of reference that office-holders serve and foster community or betray their trust. Jurisdiction and authority are important but incidental elements, means to an end. The essence and purpose of ministrial office is community.

Discussion Questions

1. What kind of community emerges from office-holders who assert their authority as the primary element in relating to people?

2. Do we find authority in the Church today closer to the secular or the New Testament model?

3. Who are some Church leaders who lead or who have led their communities as Right 17 requires?

Bibliography

Avery Dulles, MODELS OF THE CHURCH. New York: Doubleday, 1978.

Edward Schillebeeckx, THE CHURCH WITH A HUMAN FACE. New York: Crossroad, 1985.

Jean-Marie R. Tillard, THE BISHOP OF ROME. Wilmington: Michael Glazier, 1983.

18. Training Office-holders

John T. Ford, CSC

*Office-holders in the Church have the right to proper training and
fair financial support for the exercise of their offices, as well as the
requisite respect and liberty needed for the proper exercise thereof.*
(C. 231:2, C. 281)

Right 18 indicates four essential aspects in the professional life of office-holders in the Church: proper training, fair financial support, requisite respect and the need for liberty. What follows is a brief commentary
on these four aspects.

The insistence on proper training contrasts with the practice of those
ecclesiastical superiors who assign offices to subordinates who have little or no training for the ministerial responsibilities which they will be
expected to perform. While some office-holders who are appointed
without adequate preparation manage to perform surprisingly well with
"on-the-job-training," many others find themselves struggling with tasks
which they are ill-prepared to perform. In many instances, those unable
to meet the demands of such assignments not only experience physical
and mental problems in their personal lives, they frequently create difficulties for their associates. Since ministry is sufficiently challenging
even when office-holders have appropriate preparation, ecclesiastical

---

John Ford, CSC, is Associate Professor of Theology at the Catholic
University of America, Washington, DC.

superiors should take care not only to provide prospective appointees with sufficient training in advance of their appointment but also to insure that office-holders have the necessary time and means for continuing education and self-development as long as they remain in office (cf. Right 19).

Secondly, while the Church has long advocated the payment of a "living wage" to workers, among those who have been most inadequately remunerated are employees of Church-related institutions. At least in the United States, a "living wage" includes not only a salary sufficient to meet daily living expenses, but also additional benefits, such as medical insurance and retirement plans. Such benefits are necessary to prevent the recurrence of situations where some Church-workers have suddenly found themselves practically destitute as the result of extended illness, and where others, who have labored most of their working lives for the Church, reach retirement age without adequate funds to provide for their remaining years.

Many ecclesiastical office-holders are not only under-compensated but also overworked. It is all too common for Church personnel to be expected to be on constant call and to "pitch in," whatever the task of the moment. Faced with the ceaseless demands of most ecclesiastical offices, those with ministerial responsibilities need to prioritize their time and energy. Moreover, such a list of priorities should be given written expression at least in a job description, and perhaps in a legally binding contract, that stipulates what work an office-holder is expected to perform. Such a job description or contract should specify not only areas of responsibility, but also "working conditions." All too frequently, Church workers find themselves trying to work with inadequate resources under frustrating conditions. Such situations are incongruous, insofar as there is little point in employing professionally trained people if they do not have adequate working arrangements and access to appropriate resources.

Thirdly, to function well in their occupations, professional people need respect, but most of all they must respect themselves. Self-respect is closely linked to competence: Persons who are ill prepared for the positions to which they are appointed can easily succumb to a defensive attitude, which in turn proves detrimental both to their work and to their relationships with co-workers. Office-holders also need the respect of their supervisors in order to function effectively; if such respect is not accorded, one wonders why the person was appointed in the first place. Office-holders likewise need the respect of their colleagues whose help is necessary for exchanging ideas, examining proposals, and evaluating results. Similarly, office-holders need the respect of their subordinates, whose assistance is essential if proposals are to be implemented. If an office-holder is unable to perform the responsibilities connected with an office and so must be transferred or dismissed, such action should be taken with appropriate respect for the person involved, with appreciation for the service that the person has given, and with at least just, and if possible, generous compensation (cf. Right 23).

Finally, just as ministry is not assembly-line production, ministers are not interchangeable parts. If appointment to offices in the Church is based on demonstrated competence and appropriate training, then office-holders should be given ample freedom to exercise their responsibilities with originality and creativity. On the one hand, office-holders need to know the areas where they are responsible for making decisions as well as those areas where consultation or approval is required. On the other hand, ecclesiastical superiors need to realize that professionals need both encouragement and freedom in exercising their office. If ecclesiastical superiors do not have sufficient confidence in their subordinates to accord them appropriate liberty within their areas of responsibility, then again one must wonder why the appointment was made at all.

With proper training, fair financial support, requisite respect and the liberty needed to exercise their responsibilities, office-holders should be able to work more effectively and so better serve the Church and its members.

Discussion Questions

1. In your experience, has the Church been a "poor employer?" If so, why?

2. What are some success stories that would apply to Right 18?

3. Would the observance of Right 18 make "burn-out" less common among Church office-holders?

Bibliography

James Fenhagen, MINISTRY AND SOLITUDE: THE MINISTRY OF LAITY AND CLERGY IN CHURCH AND SOCIETY. New York: Seabury Press, 1981.

Sean Sammon, GROWING PAINS IN MINISTRY. Whitinsville, MA: Affirmation Books, 1983.

John Sanford, MINISTRY BURNOUT. New York: Paulist Press, 1982.

Rouch, COMPETENT MINISTRY: A GUIDE TO EFFECTIVE CONTINUING EDUCATION. Nashville-New York: Abingdon Press, 1974.

Bishops' Committee on Priestly Life and Ministry, National Council of Catholic Bishops:
THE PRIEST AND STRESS (1982)
THE CONTINUING FORMATION OF PRIESTS (1984)
THE HEALTH OF AMERICAN CATHOLIC PRIESTS (1985)

Decrees of Vatican II:
APOSTOLATE OF THE LAITY
MINISTRY AND LIFE OF PRIESTS

19. Continuing Education

John Carmody

All Catholics have the right to expect all office-holders in the Church to be properly trained and to continue their education throughout their term of office. (C. 217, C. 231:1, C. 232, C. 279, C. 819)

Ezekiel 34 is a classical statement of the responsibility religious leaders have to care for their people. 34:2 asks rhetorically, "Should not shepherds feed the sheep?" More broadly, the Hebrew prophets regularly lament the ignorance of God afflicting the Israel of their time, which ignorance they attribute to the failings of the priests and prophets. The wisdom literature abounds in calls to learn prudence and pay attention (see, e.g., Proverbs 8:5). The Johannine Jesus has Ezekiel in mind when he discourses on his own good shepherdship, in contrast to the ways of religious hirelings (see John 10:11-14), while the synoptic Jesus shows his great compassion for the people, who are like sheep without a shepherd, by teaching them (Mark 6:34, Matthew 9:35-36). The Pauline school developed the notion that missionaries ought to offer the wisdom of God (Ephesians 3:10, Colossians 1:28), and the profile of the presbyter in the Pastoral Epistles includes expending effort to develop the gifts on which ministry depends (1 Timothy 4:14-15). It is not hard, therefore, to claim that Scripture expects those who bear responsibility

---

John Carmody is a Senior Fellow in the Department of Religion at the University of Tulsa, Tulsa, OK.

for the well-being of the religious community to know their jobs and spend themselves doing their jobs well.

Most of the arguments for Right 19 simply update these biblical perspectives, in view of the function office-holders in the Church now have, in a time when many of the faithful are well-educated. To feed their sheep, show compassion to their charges, and proffer the wisdom that the good news of Christ implies, office-holders now must be learned in the things of God. They cannot be learned in the things of God unless they receive a decent education, regularly update their theological understanding, study, and pray. By the traditional ethical principle that those who want an end (here: good ministry), must effectively want the means to that end (here: education), it follows that office-holders have an obligation to keep themselves competent, and abreast of current trends.

In its decree on the ministry and life of priests, *Presbyterorum Ordinis,* Vatican II accepted this line of reasoning: "That they may be able to provide proper answers to the questions discussed by people of this age, priests should be well acquainted with the documents of the Church's teaching authority and especially of Councils and the Roman Pontiffs. They should consult, too, the best, approved writers in theological science" (19). One might wish to shift some of this language, so that the priest would not appear an answer-man and Christian wisdom would not seem so tied to Roman approval, but the call for office-holders to know what the Christian message entails and stay abreast of current intellectual trends is fully praise-worthy. The further implications include the responsibility of bishops to provide continuing education for their ministers, the responsibility of the faithful at large to support such education, and the challenge of both ministers and people to work out forums through which they may frankly and freely discuss current problems. Ultimately, all in the Church have to want a pooling of resources and a mutual stimulus to further study and prayer that make official ranks and grades less important than de facto, actual competence. Wisdom comes when all members of the Church are prompt to say, "I don't know, but I'll find out."

Discussion Questions

1. How can we use the biblical imagery of sheep and shepherds without getting trapped in undesirable, even demeaning interpretations of the roles of office-holders and general faithful?

2. What is the essential wisdom that Church-members have the right to expect in their ministers?

3. How might we get ministers and people alike to read more, broaden their horizons, and meditate on the contemporary implications of the gospel?

Bibliography

Frederick E. Crowe, S.J., OLD THINGS AND NEW: A STRATEGY FOR EDUCATION. Atlanta: Scholars Press, 1985.

Andrew Greeley et al., PARISH, PRIEST & PEOPLE. Chicago: Thomas Moore, 1981.

Edward Schillebeeckx, THE CHURCH WITH A HUMAN FACE. New York: Crossroad, 1985.

20. Academic Freedom

Leonard Swidler

Catholic teachers of theology have a right to responsible academic freedom. The acceptability of their teaching is to be judged in dialogue with their peers, keeping in mind the legitimacy of responsible dissent and pluralism of belief. (C.212:1, C.218, C.750, C.752, C.754, C.279:1, C.810, C.812)

Christian dissent in religious matters is founded in the ancient prophetic Hebraic tradition. The Hebrew prophets, of whom Jesus was one, were the Great Dissenters. Indeed, Jesus urged us on in the unending search for truth, for "the truth shall make you free" (John 8:32). As a devout Jew, Jesus valued study and teaching highly, was addressed as "teacher" (*rabbi* in Hebrew, *didaskalos* in Greek) and had his own students ("disciples," *mathetes*). Hence we find the "teachers" (*didaskaloi*) being the ones in the early Christian Church who determined the authentic Christian teaching into the latter half of the third century and again from the thirteenth century into the second half of the sixteenth century. Thomas Aquinas, for example, taught that the theologians held the "teaching chair" (*cathedra magistralis*), which conferred the right to teach (*auctoritas docendi*), and the bishops the "pastoral chair" (*cathedra pastoralis*), which conferred the right to govern (see Roger Gryson, "The Authority of the Teacher in the Ancient and Medieval

---

Leonard Swidler is Professor of Catholic Thought and Inter-Religious Dialogue at Temple University, Philadelphia, PA.

Church," in Leonard Swidler and Piet Fransen, eds., *Authority in the Church and the Schillebeeckx Case*, New York: Crossroad, 1982, pp. 176-187).

The magna carta of modern Catholic freedom of inquiry are the documents of Vatican II (1962-65): "Christ summons the Church, as she goes her pilgrim way, to that continual reformation of which she always has need . . . . Let everyone in the Church . . . preserve a proper freedom . . . even in the theological elaborations of revealed truth . . . . All are led . . . wherever necessary to undertake with vigor the task of renewal and reform . . . . [All] Catholics' . . . primary duty is to make a careful and honest appraisal of whatever needs to be renewed and done in the Catholic household itself" (Decree on Ecumenism). "The search for truth should be carried out by free enquiry . . . and dialogue . . . . Human beings are bound to follow their consciences faithfully in all their activity. . . . They must not be forced to act against their consciences, *especially in religious matters*" (Decree on Religious Liberty).

The Vatican Curia, in 1968, re-enforced this commitment to freedom and dialogue in the continual search for truth: "Doctrinal dialogue should be initiated with courage and sincerity, with the greatest freedom . . . recognizing the truth everywhere, even if the truth demolishes one so that one is forced to reconsider one's own position . . . . Therefore the liberty of the participants must be ensured by law and reverenced in practice" (*Humanae personae dignitatem*, in *Acta Apostolicae Sedis*, 60 (1968), 692-704).

The same year the U.S. National Conference of Catholic Bishops stated clearly their support for responsible dissent in the Church: "The expression of theological dissent is in order . . . . If the reasons are serious and well-founded, if the manner of dissent does not question or impugn the teaching authority of the Church, and is such as not to give scandal" (reprinted in: *National Catholic Reporter*, September 5, 1986). Cardinal Karol Wojtyla, Archbishop of Cracow in 1969, expressed a similar sentiment when he commented: "Conformity means death for any community. A loyal opposition is a necessity in any community." Finally, all this concern for theological freedom of inquiry was incorporated into the new (1983) Code of Canon Law: "Those who are engaged in the sacred disciplines enjoy a lawful freedom of inquiry and of prudently expressing their opinions on matters in which they have expertise" (Canon 218).

In the face of mounting dissent, Pope John Paul II was reported to have told the U.S. Bishops on September 16, 1987, in Los Angeles that Catholics may not in good conscience dissent from official doctrines. This report was a grave distortion of the facts. He in fact said, "It is sometimes claimed that dissent from the Magisterium is totally compatible with being a 'good Catholic'. This is a grave error."

The first thing to notice is that the pope said that it is a grave error to think that dissent is *totally* compatible with being a good Catholic, clearly implying that it *is* compatible in *some way*. In what way? A little later in his speech he explained that dissent was in fact possible as long as it was recognized not to be on the same level as the official teaching: "Dissent from Church doctrine remains what it is, dissent; as such it may not be proposed or received on an equal footing with the Church's authentic teaching." No responsible dissenter would see a difficulty in this position, for indeed s/he is expressing the dissenting position precisely in an attempt to get it accepted, eventually, as the official position.

If that were not clear enough, the pope once again reiterated the possibility of dissent (and even *confrontation*), so long as the dissenter did not make dissent an automatic, regular response to every official Church doctrine, that is, so long as dissent and confrontation were not "*a policy and a method*": "In particular your [the bishops] dialogue [with theologians] will seek to show the unacceptability of dissent and confrontation as a policy and method in the area of Church teaching."

John Paul went further and spoke of theologians' "freedom of inquiry *which is their right*"! and that the bishops must "engage in *fruitful* [not unproductive] *dialogue* with theologians." The pope emphatically proclaimed that, "I wish to support you [bishops] as . . . you rightly give them [theologians] sincere encouragement in their difficult task, and assure them how much the Church needs and deeply appreciates their dedicated and constructive work."

Discussion Questions

1. In what ways would freedom of theological inquiry promote the pursuit of truth and its most helpful expression? In what ways would its lack restrict that pursuit and expression?

2. If "the truth" is once officially formulated, may that formulation be deviated from? If so, under what circumstances, in what manner, by whom, and to what ends?

3. In searching to learn and live the truth, what are Catholics' rights and responsibilities vis a vis the Scriptures, the tradition, the magisterium, the Church community and themselves?

Bibliography

Leonard Swidler and Piet Fransen, eds., AUTHORITY IN THE CHURCH AND THE SCHILLEBEECKX CASE. New York: Crossroad, 1982.

Leonard Swidler, KUNG IN CONFLICT. New York: Doubleday, 1980.

Hans Kung and Leonard Swidler, eds., THE CHURCH IN ANGUISH: HAS THE VATICAN BETRAYED VATICAN II? New York: Harper & Row, 1987.

21. Political Matters

Edward W. Doherty

All Catholics have the right to freedom in political matters. (C. 227)

The apostolate of the social milieu, that is the effort to infuse a Christian spirit into the mentality, customs, laws and structures of the community in which a person lives is so much the duty and responsibility of the laity that it can never be properly performed by others.
—from the Decree on the Apostolate of the Laity, Second Vatican Council, §13.

Right 21 addresses the right of Catholics to carry out the "duty and responsibility" of the laity freely, i.e., to participate in the political life of their communities without interference or intimidation by the institutional Church. The Declaration on Religious Freedom of the Second Vatican Council asserted for the first time that the state should not favor one religious faith over another, thereby abandoning the Church's historic claim that the Catholic faith, as the one true faith, is entitled to the state's special protection and support. The Declaration defended the religious freedom particularly of citizens not Catholic against the claims of the state or of a state Church. Right 21, in context, espouses the freedom of citizens who *are* Catholics against attempts by officials of

---

Edward Doherty is a retired diplomat, was adviser in political affairs at the U. S. Catholic Conference and assisted in the drafting of "The Challenge of Peace."

their Church to make political decisions for them, e.g., to tell them how
to vote on issues and candidates.

Right 21 conforms to the Declaration on Religious Liberty which
noted (§ 4) "that in spreading religious faith and in introducing religious
practices everyone ought at all times to refrain from any manner of action which might seem to carry a hint of coercion."

Before a recent general election in the Federal Republic of Germany,
the president of the German bishops' conference warned Catholics not
to vote for candidates of the Green party because of that party's support
for abortion rights.

Before a recent referendum on the issue in 1986 in the Republic of
Ireland, the Irish Catholic bishops urged Catholics to vote against legislation legalizing divorce.

In the 1984 U.S. presidential campaign some U.S. bishops said
Catholics should not vote for Geraldine Ferraro, a Catholic, for vice-
president, because she did not oppose laws permitting public funding
for abortions.

Such interventions are almost always[1] a violation of the political
rights of Catholics because they do not respect the autonomy of the
political order, insisted upon by the Second Vatican Council's Pastoral
Constitution on the church in the Modern World (§ 76), which allows
the citizen to decide which policies or which candidates will best serve
the common good. Church officials have every right to address the
moral issues of public policies in sermons, pastoral letters, articles, etc.
Indeed, the political process needs these perspectives, and Catholic
citizens need them to make responsible political choices. But specific
advice on how to vote is a denial of the responsibility of the citizen and
his dignity and freedom as a person.

In the case of the Irish divorce legislation, Enda McDonagh, professor of moral theology at Maynooth, pointed out that there is a Catholic
doctrine on the indissolubility of marriage "but there is no Catholic
doctrine about having divorce legislation."[2] Similarly, there is a Catholic
doctrine on the sanctity of life which includes the human fetus, but no
Catholic doctrine on how the state can properly and effectively protect
the fetal right to life when a large part of the citizenry do not acknowledge the existence of such a right. The common good might be seen as
requiring some tolerance of this plurality of views. And Catholic
citizens and legislators can legitimately differ among themselves on how

laws—and which laws, if any—can encourage respect for fetal right to life. In this situation, the Church might better occupy itself in forming the conduct of many of its own adherents in respect of abortion, than in seeking legislation not acceptable to a large number of citizens.

Old habits die hard. During much of the early history of the Church the distinction between the temporal and the spiritual powers, as they were called, was unclear because of the breakdown of political structures following the collapse of the Roman Empire. Bishops were often also rulers of principalities or fiefdoms. With the rise of the national monarchies, the Church retreated to asserting an indirect power in temporal matters. But this claim too is now an anachronism, of which Vatican diplomacy is a remaining vestige. The term, "apostolate of the laity under the direction of the hierarchy," coined before Vatican II, is another anachronism conveying the idea that the laity must take orders from the bishops in political matters.

Increasingly, in our age, the only practicable and acceptable way for the Church to influence the domestic and external policies of nations is by persuading its adherents that policy and politics are largely about morality, and that the Church's moral teaching is supremely relevant. Bishops and theologians can define the relevant doctrines, but the rest is up to Catholic citizens whose proper freedom and autonomy Right 21 seeks to protect.

Discussion Questions

1. "Those who say religion and politics don't mix don't understand either" (Gandhi). Discuss.

2. What is the difference between Pope John Paul II's activities in Poland and Miguel D'Escoto's in Nicaragua?

3. Is voting a moral obligation?

Bibliography

J. C. Murray, WE HOLD THESE TRUTHS. New York: Sheed & Ward, 1960.

R. J. Neuhaus, THE NAKED PUBLIC SQUARE. Grand Rapids: Eerdmans, 1984.

Notes

1. Cardinal Jaime Sin's powerful intervention in the Philippines succession crisis of 1985 is probably one exception, justified by the collapse of law and order.

2. "The Church and Divorce," THE TABLET, December 13, 1986.

22. Justice and Peace

Phillip Berryman

*All Catholics have the right to follow their informed consciences
in working for justice and peace in the world* (C. 225:2).

"Action on behalf of justice and participation in the transformation
of the world," said the world's Catholic bishops at their 1971 synod,
"fully appear to us as a constitutive dimension of the preaching of the
Gospel, or, in other words, of the Church's mission for the redemption
of the human race and its liberation from every oppressive situation"
("Justice in the World" No. 6).

Although the language of the statement sounds timeless, it reflects
the result of the Church's experience of the modern world, after centuries in which Church people, by and large, have not been at the fore-
front of the struggle for justice and peace.

How does one come to an "informed conscience"? Until recently,
Catholic moral theologians tended to stress the correct application of
principles to specific circumstances. Church authorities educated consciences by teaching principles. Whatever be the merits of such a
scheme in some instances, it is clear that the struggle for justice operates
in another manner. One's conscience becomes genuinely informed only
through involvement, normally alongside others and often spurred by

---

Phillip Berryman is the author of "The Religious Roots of Rebellion"
(Orbis) and of "Liberation Theology" (Pantheon).

the prophetic acts of others. To take a well-known example, the rise of the civil rights movements can largely be traced to Rosa Parks' refusal to sit in the back of the bus. That act of conscience and the bus boycott it generated began to inform the consciences of others, including the young pastor, Martin Luther King, Jr. From action to action, from challenge to challenge, withstanding threats, intimidation, and temporizing, the movement grew until it pricked the consciences of millions of others. Catholic clergy and religious began to be visibly involved, sometimes in tension with Church authorities. Eventually the nation itself was forced to accept—at least in principle—the most basic demands of the civil rights movement.

Similarly, the pastoral letter "The Challenge of Peace" could not have occurred without many acts of conscience by individuals and small groups. In the 1950s Dorothy Day and other Catholic Worker people refused to take part in air-raid drills that would further the folly of preparing for nuclear war. Later, others dramatized war-making by pouring blood on draft files or seeking to beat missile heads into plowshares. Again, such acts of conscience normally received no encouragement from and sometimes the active opposition of Church authority.

Cardinal Maurice Roy, president of the Pontifical Commission on Justice and Peace, commenting on the tenth anniversary of "Pacem in Terris," stated that "it is the right and duty of every person to carry out a discernment between events and the moral good that they know through their consciences." Christians should discern the signs of the times and judge to what extent events are or are not in conformity with the divine plan. This discernment is not carried out in isolation but in community.

Historically and even in the present the Catholic Church has not always respected those prophets, who by their own acts of conscience, were informing the conscience of the wider Church community. Certainly not every act to which individuals feel called is in fact inspired by the Spirit. Nevertheless, Church authorities cannot themselves exercise the discernment for others. To discipline those who seek to follow their conscience in the pursuit of peace and justice is to violate their rights and to risk depriving the whole Church community of the witness it needs to come to an informed conscience.

Discussion Questions

1. How precisely do you understand the phrase "constitutive dimension" in the 1971 Synod's statement quoted at the beginning of the essay?

2. How is this right applicable at the parish level?

3. How did Jesus work for justice and peace?

Bibliography

John L. McKenzie, THE CIVILIZATION OF CHRISTIANITY. Chicago: Thomas More Press, 1986.

Francis X. Meehan, A CONTEMPORARY SOCIAL SPIRITUALITY. New York: Orbis Books, 1982.

Richard J. Cassidy, JESUS, POLITICS, AND SOCIETY. New York: Orbis Boods, 1978.

23. Working Conditions and Wages

James Biechler

All employees of the Church have the right to decent working conditions and just wages. They also have the right not to have their employment terminated without due process (C.231:2).

Justice cries out in protest, wrote Pope Leo XIII in 1891, against the force to which a worker is compelled to submit in accepting a wage lower than adequate for dignified subsistence.[1] He saw the foundation of this principle in the natural law and in Catholic theology, both of which assert the necessity of private property. Furthermore, he affirmed the natural right of workers to form associations as "the most suitable and most convenient means to attain the object proposed, which consists in this, that the individual members of the association secure, so far as possible, an increase in the goods of body, of soul, and of prosperity."[2] This Leonine teaching was the point of departure for the impressive and remarkably consistent theology of work and social justice developed by the 20th-century Church.

Pius XI referred to *Rerum Novarum* as "the *Magna Charta* upon which all Christian activity in the social field ought to be based."[3] "The worker must be paid a wage sufficient to support him and his family," he

---

James Biechler is Professor of Religion at LaSalle University, Philadelphia.

asserted.[4] In mid-century, two encyclicals of Pope John XXIII developed Catholic theology on the question of work and the rights of the working person. In *Mater et Magistra* he stated that "workers themselves have the right to act freely and on their own initiative within the above mentioned associations, without hindrance and as their needs dictate."[5] The pope gave special mention to "collective bargaining" as a means by which workers pursue their common aim. John XXIII's *Pacem in Terris*, a veritable charter of human rights, speaks of the worker's right to "working conditions in which physical health is not endangered, morals are safeguarded and young people's normal development is not impaired. Women have the right to working conditions in accordance with their requirements and their duties as wives and mothers."[6] It is from the dignity of the human person that the right derives of pursuing economic activity according to one's capacities. John XXIII then stated in unambiguous terms, adding his own special emphasis, "the worker's right to a wage is determined according to the criteria of justice. This means, therefore, one sufficient, in proportion to the available resources, to give the worker and his family a standard of living in keeping with human dignity."[7] He reaffirmed the right, based on natural law, to develop associations according to "the form they consider most suitable for the aim they have in view, and to act within such societies on their own initiative and responsibility in order to achieve their desired objectives."[8]

Vatican II underlined this teaching when it stated: "Among the basic rights of the human person is to be numbered the right of freely founding unions for working people. These should be able truly to represent them and to contribute to the organizing of economic life in the right way. Included is the right of freely taking part in the activity of these unions without risk of reprisal."[9] In his impressive letter *Laborem Exercens*, Pope John Paul II fleshed out the tradition with a profound theology of the person: Work pertains to the very essence of personhood and is not a mere means of subsistence.

Building on this rich and authoritative Catholic tradition, the bishops of the United States, in their pastoral letter "Economic Justice for All," have woven an elaborate tapestry of scripture texts, theological argumentation and social vision on the question of the right of the laborer. Citing the 1971 Synod of Bishops document "Justice in the World," they make specific application of the above principles to the Church and its agencies and state emphatically: "We bishops commit ourselves to the principle that those who serve the church—laity, clergy and religious—should receive a sufficient livelihood and the social benefits provided by responsible employers in our nation . . . . All Church institutions must also fully recognize the right of employees to organize and bargain collectively with the institution through whatever association or organization they freely choose."[10] At this stage in her history, the Church could hardly ask for a more enlightened, progressive and forthright statement in support of employee rights.

Discussion Questions

1. Why must the right to form labor unions and participate in them include the right to fashion such unions without outside interference?

2. The development of Catholic teaching on workers' rights has gone beyond concern for provision of bodily necessities to a deeper appreciation of the nature of work and its relationship to personhood. What implications might this have for the structure and function of workers' organizations?

3. What can employees of Church institutions do if their employers do not recognize their right to organize and bargain collectively?

Bibliography

Gregory Baum, THE PRIORITY OF LABOR: A COMMENTARY ON 'LABOREM EXERCENS.' New York: Paulist Press, 1982.

John C. Haughey, ed., THE FAITH THAT DOES JUSTICE. New York: Paulist Press, 1977.

Adam Maida, ed., ISSUES IN THE LABOR-MANAGEMENT DIALOGUE: CHURCH PERSPECTIVES. St. Louis, MO: Catholic Health Association of the United States, 1982.

Notes

1. RERUM NOVARUM, 63 (NCWC ed.), p. 28.
2. RERUM NOVARUM, 76 (NCWC ed.), p. 33.
3. QUADRAGESIMO ANNO, 39 (NCWC ed.), p. 16.
4. QUADRAGESIMO ANNO, 71 (NCWC ed.), p. 27.
5. MATER ET MAGISTRA, 22 (NCWC ed.), p. 9.
6. PACEM IN TERRIS, 19 (America Press ed.), p. 8.
7. PACEM IN TERRIS, 20 (America Press ed.), p. 8
8. PACEM IN TERRIS, 23 (America Press ed.), p. 9.
9. GAUDIUM ET SPES, p. 68.
10. ECOMONIC JUSTICE FOR ALL, pp. 348-349.

24. Artistic and Cultural Talents

Joseph Cunneen

All Catholics have the right to exercise their artistic and cultural talents without interference (e.g., censorship) from Church authorities; likewise all Catholics have the right freely to enjoy the fruits of the arts and culture.

When it has been most in harmony with its own richest traditions, the Church has been at home with the arts, fostering and preserving an evolving humanistic culture. After reminding us that God, in revealing himself, "has spoken according to the culture proper to different ages," *Gaudium et spes* goes on to emphasize that, "because it flows immediately from man's spiritual and social nature, culture has constant need of a just freedom if it is to develop. It also needs the legitimate possibility of exercising its independence according to its own principles" (58, 59). Hence artists and those who are striving to give expression to contemporary culture, or prepare the way for new cultural forms, must not only be free to exercise their talents on their own responsibility, but deserve the sympathetic understanding of the entire faith community as they experiment with new styles, probe the human condition, and act as advance scouts in our common effort to build a new society. Of course,

---

Joseph Cunneen is Associate Professor and Associate Chair of the Department of Philosophy and Religion at Mercy College, Dobbs Ferry, NY.

if we think of such efforts realistically, we know that some of the paths they take will prove unproductive. In addition to applying Cardinal Newman's well-known dictum that "in a sinful world we cannot expect a sinless literature," we should not expect of our contemporary artists the comprehensive vision of a modern Dante that might sum up the entire age, but try to learn from the inevitable partial insights of contemporary artists and thinkers, partial even when these makers of culture are profoundly Catholic. But their enrichment of both Church and society calls for the greatest possible freedom in the conditions in which they produce their work; such work deserves sympathetic response, thoughtful criticism, opportunities for a wise hearing, and a supportive atmosphere free of coercive pressures.

Naturally, Church authorities have not only the right but the responsibility to make informed judgments about works of art and other cultural materials intended for liturgical usage. It is in this area that the practical implementation of what *Gaudium et spes* speaks of as the "orderly freedom" which artists should enjoy (62) calls for official guidance. In matters concerning the official public worship of the Church, the individual Catholic, no matter how talented and well-intentioned, is placing his or her talent at the service of the entire Church, and the resulting work must meet special criteria if it is to enhance deepened participation in our common liturgy. Unfortunately, ecclesiastical rank is no guarantee of informed judgment in this area, and committees that commission sacred art or make decisions on materials proposed for Church use should be composed of men and women who are both theologically and aesthetically trained, with an important role reserved for working artists.

For most Catholics, their right freely to enjoy the fruits of the arts and culture is diminished and to some degree distorted to the extent that they do not regularly perceive the Church as fostering the arts and culture in all kinds of practical, everyday ways. Lay people cannot truly enter into the meaning of Scripture or participate fully in the life of the liturgy if their sense of poetry and their God-given imagination has been allowed to atrophy. To reduce the Christian mystery to a set of propositional statements and participation in the liturgy to routinized external acts results in an all but fatal loss of the interior dynamo of the symbolic structure of faith.

The Church has a significant role to play in educating Catholics to enjoy art and culture on a more profound level. Its methods can no longer include such outmoded and counter-productive approaches as placing certain books on the *Index* or condemning films or plays, but should aim at forming adult Christians who will exercise their own consciences and good taste. Probably the most significant practical way in which Church authorities can begin to implement such goals is to revamp the present education of candidates for the priesthood so that it will include far greater emphasis than at present on the training of the imagination and familiarity with contemporary culture, preferably under the guidance of lay people who are themselves distinguished critics and/or artists. Only if lay people grow up in a Church in which fearless involvement with contemporary culture and uninhibited enjoyment of the fruits of the arts are as much taken for granted as church-going itself will their rights in this area be made operative.

Discussion Questions

1. In what ways does the ordinary Catholic's everyday involvement with the local Church deepen his/her involvement with and understanding of contemporary art and culture?

2. To what degree are Catholics helped to deepen their consciousness of the symbolic structure of faith?

3. What can be done to form an atmosphere in which Catholics would instinctively support the artistic and intellectual freedom of artists and writers with whose ideology they may legitimately disagree?

Bibliography

Jacques Maritain, ART AND SCHOLASTICISM. New York: Scribner's, 1937.

John Coulson, FAITH AND IMAGINATION. New York: Oxford, 1981.

Mortimer Adler, ART AND PRUDENCE. New York: Simon & Schuster, 1941.

25. Marriage and Celibacy

Ellen O'Hara, CSJ

All Catholics have the right to choose their state in life; this includes the right to marry and the right to embrace celibacy.

In its official teaching, the Catholic Church recognizes various levels of rights: human (those arising from one's human dignity), ecclesial (those arising from one's membership in the People of God), and those arising from a particular office, ministry, or function. The right to choose one's state of life freely is an inviolable and universal human right (Pope John XXIII, *Pacem in Terris*, articles 9, 15 and 30). The documents of Vatican II also speak of basic human rights and offer, as a norm for human activity, whether or not an action enables individuals "to pursue and fulfill their total vocation" (Cf. *Gaudium et Spes*, 26, 35, 52).

The Church situates any right in relation to the common good (described in *Gaudium et Spes*, 26) and to the responsibilities and obligations flowing from the right. Historically, acknowledgment of a right has, at least theoretically, included the right to whatever is necessary to exercise the right.

The right to choose one's state of life needs to be distinguished from any guarantee that one's choice will automatically occur. What is stated is the right to choose, not a guarantee of delivery of the choice! One

---

Ellen O'Hara, CSJ, is the Director of the Marriage Tribunal for the diocese of Boise, ID.

may decide to choose marriage as one's state of life but never find anyone to marry.

Historically, the choice of state of life has not always been considered a personal right. Arranged marriages for family reasons or state alliances, and enforced entrance to a monastery or Orders have occurred. Other values in a particular society, especially where common good is seen as more important than the individual, may lead to the denial of the right or its exercise. The right under discussion here is an individual's right: The relation of the individual to a society or part of a society (e.g. clan, tribe, family) is a moral issue (in the sense of the Latin *mores*, or coming from a specific cultural and historic context), which directly affects the acknowledgment of this right. While affirming this right as both a human and an ecclesial right, it is important also to respect cultural diversity in contextualizing this right.

In order to exercise this right, an individual must have the necessary preparation, education, and opportunity. Preparation for the choice of a state of life includes an understanding of the responsibilities and obligations which correspond to the right. There is an old legal maxim which states that one cannot give what one does not have. To choose a state of life requires capacity and skills, some of which are God-given, but most of which require human sharing, modelling, training, and a certain level of basic personality development and maturity. Canon 217 says that Church members have a right to this kind of education; the Church therefore has the responsibility to provide the opportunities and training (for marriage training, c. 1065 places the responsibility on the local Christian community, not the priest).

The statement of right 25 further specifies that this right includes the right to embrace celibacy as a state or way of life. Three cautions come to mind, the first being a history of the Church's tendency, in dealing with sexuality, to exalt celibacy over marriage. Any implication that celibacy is per se a "higher" or "better" calling must be rejected, as must the implication that celibacy is automatically a lesser state than marriage. In either choice, celibacy or marriage, the potential for an introverted lifestyle, selfish, materialistic, and deaf to the cries of the world, exists. The choice of either state of life is a beginning of a call to a potentially holy life, not a guarantee of holiness.

The second caution is that either choice still demands a commitment to personal growth, concern for the Church, the rest of humanity, and the world, and the ability to participate in a healthy way in other human relationships (friendships, ministry/work, co-journeyer in prayer, etc.). The preparation of the People of God, from childhood through mature adulthood, is ongoing: An initial choice of a particular state should not cut one off from the necessary human development and appreciation of others who have chosen a different state.

The third caution is one more often associated only with marriage, but really a problem for any choice. That caution, stated in the documents of Vatican II and re-emphasized in the Code, is that there should be no coercion, direct or indirect, in the matter of a choice of lifestyle. Parents and teachers are specifically warned (*Gaudium et Spes*, 52), to avoid exerting undue influence in forcing marriage or choice of partners. (Some parents may indeed have the opposite problem—not being able to exert any influence!) The responsibility of the Church is: to provide a good preparation, without undue influence; today, this must include critical education regarding the use of media and its influence on values. As the Church becomes more participative and active in the preparation area, there will also be a corresponding understanding that, without good preparation but usually for good reasons, one's first choice of state of life may not have been a wise choice. If the critical judgment necessary for such a choice, or if the capacity to live the chosen life is not present, there must be rituals and processes for the acknowledgment of the error, and assistance in further discernment of lifestyle. The Church cannot simply penalize those who choose wrongly the first time and not assist these people through the agony of realization of the wrong choice, the transition to a different lifestyle, and the gaining of skills for a future choice.

The last part of the right is the right to marry, a natural right and an ecclesial right (C. 1058). Since marriage is a sociological and cultural phenomenon, society itself has requirements and rituals for the recognition of a marriage and the specifications of its legal effects. The basic values have to do with the stability of the society, the family, and legal relationships. Church law and teaching, especially from the time of the Council of Trent on, emphasize that the marriage of Catholics is governed also by Church law. Further, the marriage of two baptized persons (if one or both is Catholic, according to Church laws) is recognized as a sacrament (C. 1055). Church values underlying its laws are for the stability of the community, the common good, and the celebration and living of a sacrament. The underlying values of both Church and society lead both to recognize the natural right, but to restrict its exercise by establishing rules for persons entering marriage, rules for recognizing the legitimacy of the ceremony, and rules to protect those who are married (as well as procedures for terminating the marriage bond).

The question then is whether or not a Catholic has a right to marry in the Church. The answer is clearly yes. Further, when a Catholic approaches a priest or deacon to witness the marriage, the Catholic enjoys the presumption that she or he may marry, unless the pre-marital investigation reveals one of the restrictions (called "impediments") established by Church law. If an impediment exists, in most cases there are ways to remove the impediment, according to diocesan policies or Church processes.

This bears repeating: A Catholic wishing to enter marriage in the Church, and who is not burdened with any of the legally established impediments, has a right to marry and enjoys the presumption that she or he may marry in the Church. A Catholic doesn't have to prove himself or herself to the priest or deacon (or marriage team): The burden of proof is on them, if they wish to deny the right.

On the other hand, a Catholic wishing to marry is required to prepare for marriage. The remote preparation should include his/her earlier catechetical and liturgical experiences, as well as the lived family experience. Immediate preparation is also both catechetical and liturgical, with spiritual and practical components. Since the right to marry also carries with it the capacity to enter into and sustain spousal and familial responsibilities, the immediate preparation often includes some professional counseling, individually or jointly, towards such ends as communication and conflict-resolution skills and dealing with personal issues if they exist (such as abuse or alcoholism in one's background or family of origin, lack of self-esteem, etc.). The point of such assistance is not to require that people be "perfect" before they marry, but rather that their preparation be as helpful as possible. The couple who marry do so for themselves, but the health of their marriage and their participation as a couple are also a vital part of the local Christian community.

As long as marriage for Catholics requires a specific form by Church law, as long as a sacrament is involved, and as long as the Church teaches that marriage mirrors the relation of Christ and the Church (Ephesians) and is a "little church" in itself, the right will be restricted. The restriction can be in the form of delay (time specification for preparation or until some outside circumstance suspected of being a problem [e.g. young age, pregnancy, parental or societal pressure because of living together, parental desire for a marriage "in the church"] no longer exists) or in the form of denial. Either the delay or denial should be based on some objective reason grounded in Church law, not on the whim of a particular pastor or on a personality conflict. The Catholic's natural and ecclesial right to marry puts a very serious burden of proof on a minister who would delay or deny this right unjustly. A minister who makes such denials or unjust delays a practice should be penalized according to Church law for an abuse of his office.

Abuses exist on both ends of the spectrum, from deacons and priests who feel that they must marry any Catholic who wants marriage (without any preparation) to priests and deacons who rule so autocratically that their practice is to deny most Catholics who approach them or create so many "hoops" as to discourage all but the hardiest (who endure and then usually stop going to Church).

At a time when choices of a state of life are difficult, it behooves the Christian community to fulfill its responsibility to participate actively, fully, and intelligently in the preparation for and celebration of its members' choices.

Discussion Questions

1. Should there be a variety of ways for Catholics to marry, only one of which would be marriage "in the Church"? How would this affect the local Christian community?

2. On the local level, how should decisions about delaying or denying marriage of Catholics be decided?

3. In our local Christian communities, how do we prepare (remotely and immediately) our people to make choices regarding a state of life? How do we support them in their choices and mistakes?

Bibliography

Bernard Cooke, ed ALTERNATIVE FUTURES FOR WORSHIP: VOL. 5 CHRISTIAN MARRIAGE. Collegeville: Liturgical Press, 1987.

Thomas Doyle, "The Individual's Right to Marry in the Light of the Common Good," STUDIA CANONICA 13 (1979), pp. 245-301.

John F. Kinney, THE JURIDIC CONDITION OF THE PEOPLE OF GOD; THEIR RIGHTS AND OBLIGATIONS IN THE CHURCH. Rome: Catholic Book agency, 1972.

26. Equal Rights

Joan Puls, OSF

*All Catholic women have an equal right with men to the resources
and the exercise of all the powers of the Church.*

Logic would seem to imply it. Justice would seem to demand it. But
history and reality deny that the Church is a community of equals,
engaged in mutual service and mutual empowerment, committed to
human liberation and the breaking through on earth of the peace and
justice that characterize God's reign. It cannot be such a community
until women have equal access with men to the resources and powers of
that Church; until women, as well as men, administer the sacraments,
make decisions, teach, preach, heal, bless, and minister according to
their God-given gifts.

The problem does not lie in rooting this vision in Sacred Scripture.
The problem does not lie in the conflicting anthropologies that underlie
Church teaching, or in the Church's self-understanding as revealed in its
own documents. The real problem lies in the refusal of male clerics to
grant women their basic rights. It lies in the perpetuation of overt and
subtle dualisms, the guarding of historical patterns and practices, and
the actual defense and justification of sexism.

In the Old Testament it is clear that men and women were created in
God's image, that men and women were mandated as co-creators and as

---

Joan Puls, OSF, is Resource Consultant to the Generalate of the
School Sisters of St. Francis and a consultant in spirituality for the World
Council of Churches.

stewards of their surroundings, that prophecy and judgeship, spiritual and moral leadership, were entrusted to both men and women. In the New Testament we find women who possessed spiritual gifts, qualities of administrative leadership, intellectual acumen, missionary courage, and according to Paul himself, skills of articulation. Women in the gospels were believers, disciples, and trusted apostles.[1]

"Man and woman are the images of God and both in their own makeup are persons equal in dignity, endowed with the same rights. And it cannot be held in any way that woman is inferior."[2] The personhood of all human beings, as well as the affirmation of their dignity and rights, is consistently described in *Pacem in Terris, Populorum Progressio,* the Vatican II documents, and elsewhere. Likewise, the interdependence of person and community.[3] In defining itself as the people of God, the Church committed itself to the principles of participation, collegiality, and mutuality, and thereby to its identity as a community of disciples, a community of equals. Women, with men, *are* the Church, and therefore full partners in its life and mission. Partnership requires mutual service, mutual gifts, and mutual decision-making.

"Every human partnership of whatever kind is based, not on equality of gifts, but on a relationship of mutual trust, that allows each to find his or her best form of service and affirms this in others. To assume we know a person's gifts simply because of her or his biological sex is a form of 'heresy,' because the Spirit works in many ways through people."[4] Baptism (and not Holy Orders) ushers us into the Christian life, the Church, the community of equals. As vital members of the body of Christ, we all share in the resources and the powers of that body.[5] Our roles, our responsibilities, our relationships, flow from that premise and not from gender, historical models, or existing systems of power and authority. Because we are members of the body, a priestly people, we bless, teach, forgive, ordain one another. We are a community of believers, not a society of classes and castes.

"All of you who have been baptized into Christ have clothed yourselves with him. There does not exist among you Jew or Greek, slave or free-person, male or female. All are one in Christ Jesus. Furthermore, if you belong to Christ, you are descendants of Abraham [and Sarah], which means you inherit all that was promised."[6] Women today are claiming their rightful inheritance. Concern for their dignity and full equality is a human rights' concern and it is felt around the world. The

Church's credibility in its espousal of human rights rests on its credibility as guarantor and guardian of the rights of its own members. Women are human, and humans have rights. Gender cannot disqualify anyone from access to the rights stemming from baptism. Consultation can no longer substitute for decision-making power. Passivity cannot continue to pass for participation. Double standards and discrimination in any segment or activity of the Church cannot disguise themselves as justice.

In the end, the problem is one of conversion, from our male-centered, hierarchically-structured idolatries. Then we can recommit ourselves to our identity as Christians disciples, reconciled, and mutually related. Only then will we be faithful to the spirit and mandate of the gospel. And only then will we all minister to the needs and longings of the whole people of God. Only then will we be a credible sign of the coming of the reign of God.

Discussion Questions

1. How do we begin to convert both attitudes and behavior so that they reflect the truth of our common membership "in the body" and our right to exercise God-given gifts?

2. Can we envision some of the benefits and blessings which might flow from "a community of equals" in the Church?

Bibliography

Elisabeth Fiorenza, IN MEMORY OF HER: A FEMINIST THEOLOGICAL RECONSTRUCTION OF CHRISTIAN ORIGINS. New York: Crossroads, 1983.

Rosemary Radford Reuther, SEXISM AND GOD-TALK: TOWARD A FEMINIST THEOLOGY. Boston: Beacon Press, 1983.

Letty M. Russell, HUMAN LIBERATION IN A FEMINIST PERSPECTIVE. Philadelphia: Westminster, 1974.

Notes

1. Genesis 1: 27-8; Joel 3:1-2, Exodus 15:19-21; II Kings 22; Judges 4:4-9; Luke 8:1-3, 40-56; Matt. 15:21-28; Luke 24:1-11; John 4; John 20:11-18; Acts 9:36-42; Acts 16:13-15, 40; Acts 18; Philippians 4:2-3; Romans 16:1-16.

2. Pope Pius XII, Sept. 29, 1957, LA DOCUMENTATION CATHOLIQUE, Vol. 54, No. 1263, col. 1352.

3. PACEM IN TERRIS, 9ff; POPULORUM PROGRESSO 15; GAUDIUM ET SPES 24-26, 29.

4. Letty M. Russell, "Theological Aspects of Women and Men in Christian Communities," BULLETIN INTERNATIONAL DES FEMMES ET HOMMES DANS L'EGILSE, No. 17, Avril, 1976, p. 7.

5. LUMEN GENTIUM, 12, 31-33.

6. Galatians 3:27-29.

27. Church Resources

J. Patrick Murphy, CM

All Catholics have the right to expect that the resources of the Church be fairly expended on their behalf without prejudice to race, age, nationality, sex, sexual orientation, state-of-life, or social position.

Most people assume that Right 27 is self-evident. The assessment that the collective owners of specified resources must have those resources expended on and for the purposes of the owners is plain enough. That it should apply to the Church and its agencies is equally clear.

We know that membership in the Church is conferred at baptism. At that time access to a fair share of the resources of the Church is offered. Both elements, access and fair share, are essential. The Church validates these assertions by firmly grounding them in social theory and the documents of Vatican II as well as by contemporary papal and episcopal writings.

From organizational theory we know that communities are formed on the basis of reciprocity of habitualized actions. The important concept here is that actions are *reciprocal.* People join organizations to both achieve organizational goals and satisfy individual needs. Furthermore, shared actions built up over time create a history, which in turn tends to

---

J. Patrick Murphy, CM, is Associate Professor in the Public Services program at DePaul University, Chicago, IL.

control human conduct, predefining patterns of behavior. When reciprocity fails—it can happen in any organization—the organization is threatened and the quality of life of people decays. Individual needs are not met. Similarly, when resources are no longer spread among members fairly, the organization deteriorates and its goals are not met. During times when resources are short it is even more critical that members monitor who distributes the resources and on what basis.

We usually think of Church resources as either spiritual, such as grace, or temporal, such as the physical plant and money. Considering only temporal resources, they also include personnel, information, education, time spent on task, office or position of power, and participation in decision-making.

We fail the obligation of fair expenditure of Church resources, thereby committing the sins of discrimination, (a) when we distribute resources in unequal ways, (for instance by paying differing stipends or salaries to clergy, religious, and lay people for equivalent work), (b) when we exclude some members from distribution (for instance, when a woman is paid less or offered fewer benefits because her husband is already employed), (c) when we bias our evaluations of need or performance for some members, (for instance by assuming that mothers will be absent from jobs more than fathers), and (d) when we deny access to status or productivity-enhancing activities to some, but not all, (such as budgeting for professional development and spiritual retreats for priests but not for professional lay staff) (Murphy, 1985).

The sociological perspective is further supported by a sense of justice. If there is no socialization there is not sharing. Where there is no sharing there can be no Church. Gospel justice demands that social institutions be ordered in a way that guarantees all persons the ability to participate actively in the economic, political and cultural life of society. Such participation is an essential expression of the social nature of human beings and of their communitarian vocation. These ideas flow from the two principles of social solidarity and participation. Moreover, the bishops have called themselves to internal justice and committed themselves to the principles that those who serve the Church—laity, clergy, and religious—should receive a sufficient livelihood and the social benefits provided by responsible employers in the United States. These are bold statements and ones that will require hard work to deliver what they intend (*Economic Justice for All*, 78, 187, 188, 347, 351).

Right 27 and its essential arguments pressure all levels and functions of the Church: the Vatican or international perspective, the diocesan or regional perspective, and the parish or local community. The fact that the Church has a special relationship with its members because its leaders are entrusted with their spiritual welfare is even more sobering. The danger of betraying the spiritual trust because of betrayed temporal trust is serious. In today's environment, this obligation to provide for fair allocation of Church resources becomes ever more imperative.

Discussion Questions

1. For dioceses: Are the resources of time and financial support for retreats and professional development fairly distributed among clergy ministers and non-clergy ministers by policy? In practice? Per capita, are the financial and human resources provided to poor parishes comparable to the same resources provided to more affluent parishes? Are some groups systematically excluded from sharing in the gifts and resources of the diocese (e.g. gay people and divorced Catholics)?

2. For parishes: Are the compensation packages for clergy, lay and religious comparable? Are some groups short-changed when it comes to providing services and resources: Singles? Elderly? Children? Adults? Minorities? Gays? Divorced?

3. For individuals or managers. Draw a pie chart of sources of income or resources. Draw another of expenditures of resources. Do they make sense in light of justice and Right 27?

Bibliography

J. Patrick Murphy, CM, "Sexism in the Church, A Personnel Perspective," PROFESSIONAL DEVELOPMENT PUBLICATION. Cincinnati: National Association of Church Personnel Administrators, 1985.

National Association of Church Personnel Administrators, JUST TREATMENT FOR THOSE WHO WORK FOR THE CHURCH. Cincinnati: National Association of Church Personnel Administrators, 1986.

NCCB, ECONOMIC JUSTICE FOR ALL: CATHOLIC SOCIAL TEACHING AND THE US ECONOMY. 1986.

P. L. Berger, and T. Luckmann, THE SOCIAL CONSTRUCTION OF REALITY. Garden City, NY: Doubleday, 1967.

Barbara Garland, SC, COMPENSATION: A MANUAL FOR ADMINISTRATION OF CHURCH SYSTEMS. Cincinnati: National Association of Church Personnel Administrators, 1987.

27a. Religious Education of Children

Denise Lardner Carmody

All Catholic parents have the right to expect fair material and other assistance from Church authorities in the religious education of their children.

This right assumes that Christian parents and church authorities should be allies, positive collaborators, in the education of youth. When we seek biblical perspectives on this matter, such texts as Deuteronomy 6 and Proverbs 1 leap to mind as reminders of the great store that Israel set on the proper upbringing of the next generation. Thus, after the *shema*, the great call that summarizes Israelite monotheism, we read: "You shall teach them [these words] to your children, and shall talk of them when you sit down in your house, and when you walk by the way, and when you lie down, and when you rise." Proverbs 1, which purports to be part of the legacy of Solomon, the prototype of Israelite wisdom, includes the thematic lines, "Hear, my child, your father's instruction, and reject not your mother's teaching" (1:8). When one adds the prophetic commonplace that the people will be ignorant of God unless they have wise, energetic priests and prophets, one sees that Right 27a has a solid foundation in the Hebrew Bible.

Denise Carmody is Chairperson of the Department of Religion at the University of Tulsa, Tulsa, OK.

The New Testament offers similarly powerful perspectives on the importance of the religious education of children. At the conclusion of the Lukan infancy narrative, we see the child Jesus sitting among the teachers in the temple, "listening to them and asking them questions" (2:46). The onlookers are astonished at his understanding, and he leaves the temple to return home and increase "in wisdom and in stature, and in favor with God and man" (2:52)—not a bad summary of what Christian parents should hope for their children. The evangelists frequently portray Jesus as drawn to children and kindly toward them (e.g., Mark 9:36-37, Matthew 19:13-14, John 4:46-54). Paul includes in the profile of the good Jew the phrase, "a teacher of children" (Romans 2:20), while Hebrews 2 details the solidarity between Jesus, the pioneer of our salvation, and those he saves, in a figure of parenting: "Here am I, and the children God has given me" (2:13). Therefore, despite its eschatological expectations, the New Testament values children and parenting enough to make them prime foci of God's care to communicate divine life.

The decree of Vatican II on Christian education, *Gravissimum educationis*, is explicit that all people have an inalienable right to education (1), that every Christian is entitled to a Christian education (2), and that parents should get help in educating their children: "While belonging primarily to the family, the task of imparting education requires the help of society as a whole" (3). The argument that Christian parents have the right to material and other assistance from Church authorities in this matter has the logic of *a fortiori*: If secular society has the obligation to assist in the education of the next generation, so much the more do the Church and its authorities. Secular society presumably will be shrewd enough to realize that the future prosperity of any people and culture depends on the excellent preparation of the next generation of citizens. Few tasks are more crucial to the common good than this one, so we may judge a given society by the priority it gives to the education of its youth. This criterion completely holds for the Christian Church, where one might expect the further realization that children are a gift of God to the entire community, not just to their biological parents. From this realization it follows that all Catholic parents have the right to expect aid from all members of the Church, according to the resources and opportunities of each.

Discussion Questions:

1. What does the quotation from Deuteronomy suggest about religious education in the home?

2. What does the scene of the child Jesus in the Temple suggest is the proper goal of Christian religious education?

3. How might the Pauline notion of the Body of Christ spotlight the obligations all Christians have toward the education of the next generation?

Bibliography

Thomas H. Groome, CHRISTIAN RELIGIOUS EDUCATION. San Francisco: Harper & Row, 1980.

Kathleen and James McGinnis, PARENTING FOR PEACE AND JUSTICE. Maryknoll, NY: Orbis, 1981.

Brian Wren, EDUCATION FOR JUSTICE. Maryknoll, NY: Orbis, 1977.

27b. Resources for Single Catholics

Sonya A. Quitslund

All single Catholics have the right to expect that the resources of the Church be fairly expended on their behalf.

The Notre Dame Study of U.S. Parishes Today indicates that between 31 percent and 44 percent of adults (18 and over) attending Mass are single (never married, separated, divorced and not remarried, or widowed). Fifty-seven percent of Catholics under 30 have not yet married.[1] Moreover, there is a substantial decline in Mass attendance after age 70. The single, widowed and married attend Mass at least twice as often as the separated and divorced.[2]   Are Church resources being expended equitably for the spiritual needs of the single Catholic?   While it is difficult to make broad generalizations, most would argue parochial schools absorb a disproportionate share of parish finances.   Some, but not all statistics, support this.[3]

To determine an equitable share for single Catholics we must decide not only their needs but also consider parish priorities.   Ought parishes set aside between 31 and 44 percent of the budget to provide services for single people?   How do we determine which single people receive these

---

Sonya Quitslund is Associate Professor of Religious Studies, George Washington University, Washington, DC.

services? Only dues-paying members? Only those who attend Mass regularly? Only those officially registered? The statistics cited above focused on people attending Mass but excluded Hispanics.[4] They included no data on membership or contributions. Many pastors complain single people either do not attend or do not contribute—money or talents. Single people complain parishes are too family-oriented; that pastors fail to address both their spiritual and social needs.

But deeper issues than questions of who is right and who is wrong are at stake. Are contributions to the Church, whether in time, talent or money, to be viewed as investments from which we have a right to expect some return? In short, are contributions a form of alms or the purchase of services? Is the Church just a social club or a department of social services? How do we address the needs of single people 18 and over? Obviously multiple programs would be necessary. But is this the primary purpose of the parish?

Since the Bible tells us how the People of God were originally called into existence, it ought to offer some clues and guidance in defining the purpose of this community of believers. The first thing we discover in the Hebrew Scriptures is that the single state was not promoted. Procreation was a divine mandate; polygamy helped ease the situation of surplus women. There is, however, an ever-present concern for one group of singles: widows. People were expected to tithe as a matter of course. Every third year the tithe was set aside to provide specifically for the "alien, orphan and widow" (Dt 26:12). (Dt 27:19 is the strongest pre-Christian statement: "Cursed is he who distorts the justice due an alien, orphan and widow.") The Bible makes it clear the widow has a right to have her material needs cared for out of the surplus of the community.

The New Testament offers some new developments. First of all, singleness is now an acceptable, even a superior mode of life (Mt 19:12; 1 Cor 7:8.) But it is to be espoused primarily to work for the Kingdom. Jesus himself redefined neighbor in a most radical way in Lk 10, as the nearest person in need, and made effective response to these needs the basis for entry into the Kingdom (Mt 25:31-46). The communal lifestyle of the early Jerusalem Christians had as its motivation to see that all were provided for equitably, but almost from the start there were complaints. Deacons were duly appointed to monitor a just distribution (Acts 6:23). This admirable idealism had already been marred in Acts 5 when Ananias and Sapphira fell victim to their concern for old age security and the community's need for honesty.

On the basis of biblical imperatives, it would seem the initial answer to the issue of how Church funds are to be expended rests solely on where the greatest need is perceived. The parable of the Good Samaritan (Lk 10) adds a new dimension, suggesting that if non-Catholics somewhere in the world are in greater need than parish members, they ought to be the primary recipients, not the parishioners, whether single or married.

The more one searches scripture for a clue, the more it seems the whole financial structure and priorities of the Church need to be re-examined. What is the first priority? A building, a school? If we take the prophetic teaching on justice, "sedaqa," as having any relevance for Catholics today, we find that the sin for which the people were condemned was lack of faithfulness to the community, more popularly expressed today as lack of social justice. These charges came at a time when temple-cult was flourishing, almost as much as the crimes of inhumanity. For the prophets, the purpose of religion was to promote "healthy human existence," an existence willed by God that could only find its wholeness in community.

We read nothing (in Paul) about assessments for church buildings or for entertaining traveling church dignitaries. But already in the 50s, Christians were educated to think of the poor. Paul urged all his Gentile communities, most of whom were poor, to set aside money to help the poor—not in their own towns, but in Jerusalem! This sign of human solidarity was crucial to his theology of the Body of Christ and the Christian's understanding of what it meant to be "in Christ"—no longer Jew nor Greek, free nor slave, male nor female (Gal 3:28). One custom he strongly denounced was that of "agape"—a church pot-luck supper—precisely because as practiced, it failed to promote community (1 Cor 11:17, 20-22).

The primary goal of the parish is therefore the creation of a community experience in which all, single and married, young and old, male and female, can find their life enhanced and enriched. Money spent that does not promote this is money ill-spent. Perhaps single Catholics do not support the parish because they object to how funds are spent. Perhaps they are not seen around the church because they do not find a community spirit; instead they encounter closed cliques. Perhaps they agree with Trito-Isaiah that it is inappropriate to spend money and energy building new buildings when the body of Christ is fractured by divisions, by disregard of human rights and needs (Is 58:66). Perhaps when parishes develop a global sense and make the hard financial decisions this demands, single people will feel more at home.[5]

The question is not therefore whether single Catholics have the right to expect that the resources of the Church be fairly expended on their behalf, but that they be expended according to he guidelines of scripture. Certainly the laborer is worthy of his hire (Lk 10:7) but this applies as much to the lay people as to the clerics that serve the community. Obviously a modest parish plant must be maintained. But every penny need not go back into the plant, nor need large bank accounts be built up for future emergencies when the Body of Christ lies broken and bleeding around the world.

The 1971 Synod on Justice clearly recognized that the Church is bound to give witness to justice, but that to do so, it must first be just in the eyes of the world. Moreover, the bishops reiterated the recommendations that lay people should exercise more important functions with regard to Church property, and should share in its administration.[6]

Yes, all single Catholics have the right to expect that the resources of the Church be fairly expended on their behalf. But this does not mean the resources will be spent directly on their own spiritual or social needs. Some will always have greater needs than others and part of the example of Jesus was to do without even the essentials so that he could expend himself more totally for the needs of others (Mt 8:20).

If being single was viewed as a problem in ancient Israel, it was seen as sign of a special calling in the New Testament, underlined with the challenge to "Go, sell what you have, give to the poor . . . and then come follow me" (Lk 18:22). The final word for the single person is: "Ask not what the Church can do for you, but what you can do for the Church— not only in terms of generous contributions, but in spiritual contributions, whether of active ministry or simply of prayer, as well as in leading the Church to greater fiscal responsibility.

Discussion Questions

1. Are contributions to the Church an investment from which single Catholics have a right to expect some return? Is our giving contingent upon what we receive?

2. Should tithing be adopted by the Catholic Church? Is tithing the same as almsgiving? What is the single Catholic's moral obligation in this regard?

3. Should religious education focus on rights or responsibilities? Should Mt 25:31-46 or the 10 commandments and 6 precepts of the Church be the basis for Christian morality?

Bibliography

BIBLE.

THE N.D. STUDY OF US PARISHES TODAY. University of Notre Dame, Indiana, 1986.

ORIGINS, Vol. 14, pp. 459f, 670f; Vol. 15 #4, pp. 49-57; #20 pp. 329-340; #37, pp. 611-616; #45 pp. 733-744; vol. 16 #11 pp. 206-216.

Notes

1. ORIGINS vol. 14, 1984, p. 675. One-fourth to one-third of American Catholics do not have parish connections and a NORC general survey of Catholics indicates that 34 percent rarely attend Mass, cf. ORIGINS vol. 15, p. 52.

2. Ibid., vol. 15, p. 55.

3. In Cleveland, 80 percent of a parish budget goes to the school, 10 percent to the parishioners, the rest presumably goes for diocesan collections, U.S. CATHOLIC vol. 52, no. 1, 1987, p. 41. A large suburban Maryland parish estimates 45 percent of the budget supports the parish school, The Washington, DC archdiocesan Office of Education claims parishes spend approximately 33 percent of their budgets on schools, but the archdiocese spends more than half of its budget on education—52 percent.

4. For two main reasons: 1) cost of administering and producing a bilingual instrument; 2) marked cultural between Hispanic and non-Hispanic parishes. The NORC study gives a higher percentage of singles, many of whom are no longer actively in parish life.

5. NCR 3/27/87 "Some say Peter's Pence robs Peter to Pay John Paul," p. 21. A Milwaukee pastor allowed his people to designate where they wanted their Peter's Pence money to go. $1700 was designated to go to Third World charities, $300 to the pope.

6. cf nos. 40 and 41 of this document "Justice in the World."

28. Family Planning

Sidney Callahan

All married Catholics have the right to determine in conscience the size of their families and the appropriate methods of family planning.

Family planning is a relatively new responsibility for married Christians. Within the last fifty years there has been an explosion of medical and scientific knowledge about human reproduction. The same forces of scientific progress which reduce infant mortality now give modern couples the capacity to control their fertility. With these new powers come unavoidable responsibilities, with corresponding rights. To ignore this potential for birth regulation is to make a decision not to decide— and can a Christian in conscience ignore God's gift of responsible control over nature?

Married persons have the right to make these procreative decisions, for it is by their actions that a new life will, or not, come into the world. They will be accountable to God for their exercise of procreative powers, which the vocation of marriage entails. Christian parents are also responsible for rearing the children that they procreate, so a decision to have a child ordinarily includes the long-term commitment of personal resources. Such a serious life decision requires prudence as

---

Sidney Callahan is Associate Professor of Psychology at Mercy College, Dobbs Ferry, NY.

well as faith and trust: Those who will be responsible for the consequences have the right to make this decision.

As the Vatican II document *Gaudium et Spes* teaches, married persons enter into the "conjugal covenant" and by their mutual bestowal of consent and acceptance there arises the relationship of marriage, in accordance with God's will. Thus, "by their very nature, the institution of matrimony itself and conjugal love are ordained for the procreation and education of children." While marriage is not instituted solely for procreation, but also for marital love, mutual healing and mutual perfection, the responsibility for procreative decisions is clear: "The parents themselves should ultimately make this judgment, in the sight of God." Married Catholics have the right and responsibility to make their judgments, "governed according to a conscience dutifully conformed to the divine law itself" (*Gaudium et Spes*, 50).

Controversies have since arisen over which methods of family planning are in accord with the divine law. Obviously, a Catholic could not determine with an informed conscience that infanticide was an appropriate method of family planning, even if it has been customary in many cultures. Appropriate methods for a Catholic can only include methods which control fertility by means other than killing an individual human life in or out of the womb. Arguments over fertility regulation have been partially dominated by the question of whether a particular method is a form of early abortion.

Methods relying on sexual abstinence during the fertile period have been accepted by all as appropriate since they cannot be abortifacients and have other advantages. These methods use knowledge of conception to control the reproductive process and avoid intrusive methods with all their dangers of side effects. They require the education and mutual cooperation of spouses so that marital unity and love is enhanced. Complete respect is given to the reproductive potential of marital sexuality.

In many circumstances, however, only medically more intrusive methods of birth control can be used reliably. The decision then becomes whether the unity and love engendered by sexual intercourse is more important than the value of having each individual sexual act open to its full reproductive potential. Many, many Catholics, including many theologians, have held that the well-being of persons and the need to strengthen the marriage and family as a whole, are more important than the reproductive integrity of each sexual act. When used for the right reasons, artificial contraceptives which are not abortifacients, have been viewed as an acceptable choice. These principles were well articulated by the final report of the Papal Commission on birth control set up by Pope Paul VI, a commission consisting of theologians, bishops and lay persons. "The morality of sexual acts between married people takes its meaning first of all specifically from the ordering of their actions in a fruitful married life, that is one which is practiced with responsible generous and prudent parenthood. It does not then depend upon the direct fecundity of each and every particular act. Moreover the morality of every marital act depends upon the requirements of mutual love in all its aspects."

The Commission's report goes on to succintly describe the changes which have helped develop the Church's affirmation of marital sexuality:

The reasons in favor of this affirmation are of several kinds: social changes in matrimony and the family, especially in the role of the woman; lowering of the infant mortality rate; new bodies of knowledge in biology, psychology, sexuality and demography; a changed estimation of the value and meaning of human sexuality and of conjugal relations; most of all a better grasp of the duty of [human beings] to humanize and to bring to greater perfection for the life of [human beings] what is given in nature. Then must be considered the sense of the faithful; according to it, condemnation of a couple to a long and often heroic abstinence as the means to regulate conception, cannot be founded on the truth.

A further step in the doctrinal evolution, which it seems now should be developed, is founded less on these facts than on a better, deeper and more correct understanding of conjugal life and of the conjugal act when these other changes occur. The doctrine on marriage and its essential values remains the same and whole, but it is now applied differently out of a deeper understanding.

This report represents for many an authentic guide for the informed conscience of Catholics.

Discussion Questions:

1. How does marital sexuality strengthen the goals of Christian marriage and family life?

2. What makes it difficult for Christians in the modern world to take a Christian view of sexuality and family life?

3. What factors should married persons take into account as they in conscience decide on family size or on methods of family planning?

Bibliography

GAUDIUM ET SPES, Vatican Council II Documents.

John Noonan, CONTRACEPTION. Cambridge, MA: Harvard University Press, 1965.

Robert Blair Kaiser, THE POLITICS OF SEX AND RELIGION: A CASE HISTORY IN THE DEVELOPMENT OF DOCTRINE, 1962-1984. Kansas City, MO: Leaven Press, 1985.

Anthony Kosnik, William Carroll, Agnes Cunningham, Ronald Modras, James Schulte, HUMAN SEXUALITY: NEW DIRECTIONS IN AMERICAN CATHOLIC THOUGHT, A Study Commissioned by The Catholic Theological Society of America. New York: Paulist Press, 1977.

29. Parents Educating Children

Rodger Van Allen

All Catholic parents have the right to see to the education of their children in all areas of life (C. 226:2).

Right 29 in the Charter speaks clearly of parental rights in the education of their children. Canon 226:2, which is explicitly cited, states: "Because they have given life to their children, parents have a most serious obligation and enjoy the right to educate them; therefore Christian parents are especially to care for the Christian education of their children according to the teaching handed on by the Church." This canon was drawn principally from Vatican II's document on education, *Gravissimum educationis*, 3, a key portion of which states: "Since parents have conferred life on their children, they have a most solemn obligation to educate their offspring. Hence, parents must be acknowledged as the first and foremost educators of their children." This passage includes references to the papal encyclicals *Divini illius magistri* (1929) and *Mit brennender Sorge* (1937) that have reflected the Church-state concerns that have been an important part of this defense of parental rights. *Divini illius magistri* explicitly quotes the U.S. Supreme Court decision in the Oregon School Case, June 1, 1925: "The fundamental theory of

---

Rodger Van Allen is Professor of Religious Studies at Villanova University, Philadelphia, PA.

155

liberty upon which all governments in this Union repose excludes any general power of the State to standardize its children by forcing them to accept instruction from public teachers only. The child is not the mere creature of the State; those who nurture him and direct his destiny have the right, coupled with the high duty, to recognize and prepare him for additional duties." With similar thinking, Pope Leo XIII in 1890 in *Sapientiae christianae*, 42, maintained that parents "hold from nature their right of training the children to whom they have given birth."

In and since Vatican II more attention has been given to the spiritual and psychological dimensions of these parental rights and responsibilities. Especially notable is the discussion of the family as "the domestic church" (*Lumen gentium*, 11). This reactivated a traditional description of the Christian family that was present in the early centuries of the Church. Pope Paul VI's encyclical on evangelization, *Evangelii nuntiandi*, 71, stated that understanding the family as the domestic Church "means that there should be found in every family the various aspects of the entire Church." Thus the family is to be an evangelizing community, a worshiping community, and a ministerial community. This is a promising and creative theology for a renewal of Christian family life and society.

Another encouraging development concerns the dawning awareness of some corollaries of the long time emphasis on parental rights in education. As Lorraine P. Amendolara states in *Momentum*, the journal of the National Catholic Education Association, "If Catholic educators truly respect the parent as the primary educator, the attitudes and policies toward parental involvement in the child's education must change." She points out that in the past, in actuality, "many administrators have held parents and parent organizations at bay, fearing intrusion." Parents, teachers and administrators need to view one another as partners not adversaries. All parties "have a serious duty to commit themselves totally to a cordial and active relationship" says Pope John Paul II in *Familiaris consortio*, 40.

A final thought: parents can sometimes err through a zealousness to make their children into achievers in all kinds of endeavors. In extreme situations, children become used in a none too subtle way to gratify parental egos. It is useful to review the words of Ephesians 1:4, "And parents, never drive your children to resentment, but, in bringing them up, correct them and guide them as the Lord does."

Discussion Questions

1. What rights does the state have in education?

2. Are there more reasons or fewer reasons for respecting parental rights in Catholic institutions or public institutions?

3. How does an appreciation of the family as the "domestic Church" build partnerships in education within the Church?

Bibliography

Lorraine P. Amendolara, "Are Parents a Part of Your Education Community?" MOMENTUM, December 1984, pp. 56-57.

David M. Thomas, FAMILY LIFE AND THE CHURCH. New York: Paulist Press, 1979.

Pope John Paul II, FAMILIARIS CONSORTIO (Community of the Family), November 22, 1981, especially paragraphs 36-41.

30. Divorce and Remarriage

William T. More, SCJ

All married Catholics have the right to withdraw from a marriage which has irretrievably broken down. All such Catholics retain the radical right to remarry.

Rights always have to be seen in the context within which they are to be exercised. A right to drive a motor vehicle is conditioned in its exercise by age and a driver's license. A right to marry is conditioned by the laws of the land and government pertaining to marriage. Likewise, there are rules and regulations concerning marriage for those who want to exercise their right to marry within the context of the Church.

Since rules and regulations may change from time to time, it does not follow that rules and regulations of a certain time are necessarily the best for that particular period of time.

When a marriage has irretrievably broken down a person has the right and often the duty to separate himself or herself from a situation that only leads to destruction. A Christian is called to life and to life in abundance (Jn. 10:20). Nowhere in Christian teaching or in the Bible is it said that anyone is called to destruction.

Therefore, a person who separates himself or herself from an untenable situation, and does so after having tried other solutions, exer-

---

William More, SCJ, is Director of the Office of Family Ministry and of the Ministry of Separated and Divorced Catholics in the Archdiocese of Ottawa, Canada.

cises his or her right to survival—which may mean physical, mental, emotional or spiritual survival. Even a Church which upholds the indissolubility of marriage honors such a basic human and Christian principle. No one is held to the impossible.

The right to remarry is also conditioned in its exercise by certain laws. The civil law requires that the previous marriage first be dissolved by a civil divorce. In addition to the civil divorce, Church laws require that a declaration of nullity be granted before one can remarry in the Roman Catholic Church. Every formerly married Roman Catholic or any non-Roman Catholic wishing to remarry in the context of the Roman Catholic Church, has the right to investigate the possibility of obtaining from the Roman Catholic Church a declaration of nullity of his/her former marriage.

When Jesus spoke about divorce and remarriage in his time (Mt. 5:32), he seemed to allow for divorce and remarriage at least on one ground. On the other hand, he also preached the indissolubility of marriage.

Marriage and remarriage are not private matters; society or the community has something to say about them. The right to remarry can, therefore, never be a private matter either or an absolute right without any conditions or regulations.

While Christ upheld the indissolubility of marriage on the one hand, he was most compassionate and merciful to those who could not always live up to all the demands of the law. If the Church is to be true to Christ, it must likewise, follow Christ in these aspects. The Church must also continue its further research into the ways and means the conditions for remarriage are arrived at, so that through the Church, Christ's mercy and compassion becomes more and more visible.

Discussion Questions

1. Since there is so much confusion about the conditions that the Church has laid down for someone who wants to remarry in the Roman Catholic Church, what is the present legislation of the Church in this matter?

2. What positive suggestions would you have with regard to the present legislation so that the Church becomes more and more reflective of Christ's mercy and compassion?

3. Freedom to remarry does not equate readiness for remarriage. What necessary steps do you think have to be taken in this process of preparing for remarriage in order to give this new marriage enough viability to survive?

Bibliography

Victor J. Pospishil, DIVORCE AND REMARRIAGE. New York: Herder and Herder, 1967, 203 pp.

Steven Preister, and James J. Young, CATHOLIC REMARRIAGE, PASTORAL ISSUES AND PREPARATION MODELS. Mahwah, NJ: Paulist Press, 1986, 196 pp.

James J. Young, ed., MINISTERING TO THE DIVORCED CATHOLIC. New York: Paulist Press, 1979, p. 259.

31. Sacraments for Divorced and Remarried

Sally Cunneen

All Catholics who are divorced and remarried and who are in conscience reconciled to the Church have the right to the same ministries, including all sacraments, as do other Catholics.

The constant responsibility of Church authorities to provide wise regulations for pastoral care and the administration of the sacraments must always serve its primary goal: "that all the faithful of Christ of whatever rank or status are called to the fullness of the Christian life and to the perfection of charity" (*Lumen Gentium,* 40). The beautifully charged language of this document goes on to emphasize that, for our growth in love, "Each must share frequently in the sacraments, the Eucharist especially" (42). Contemporary theological renewal on the subject of the sacraments, emphasizing them as "encounters" with Christ— "by his power He is present in the sacraments" (*Sacrosanctum Concilium,* 7)—should establish a general understanding that, although it could well be said that none of us has a *right* to the sacraments, they are to be made as available as possible to all the faithful. Although the traditional ideal of indissoluble Christian marriage should be put before us,

---

Sally Cunneen is a Professor in the English Department of Rockland Community College and a founding editor of *Cross Currents* magazine.

in season and out of season, the pastoral needs of divorced and remarried Catholics are not therefore to be sacrificed.

Examples taken from Jesus' own ministry make clear that the Church is to provide a total ministry to all who seek it. The Master who ate with tax-collectors and others who were considered public sinners, who offered himself as living water to the Samaritan woman, surely does not wish to have us treat the divorced and remarried as second-class members of his Body. The sacraments are not prizes for those who have earned them, but signs of God's nurturing care for all those who acknowledge their weakness yet wish to be united to Jesus. Fortunately, the official ministry to separated and divorced Catholics has made great progress in the United States in recent years, and the climate of understanding has improved dramatically since the penalty of excommunication for a second marriage "outside the Church" was removed in 1977. Since then, as the late Father James Young, National Chaplain of the North American Conference of Separated and Divorced Catholics reminded us, "There is no penalty in law which excludes the divorced and remarried from the Eucharist."

At the same time, just as none of us should dare to say "Our Father" in a mechanical or frivolous manner, we all need to be reminded to approach the sacraments with great reverence. For example, the Church has been increasingly insistent that parents should realize that Baptism is not to be regarded as a purely social custom but to commit themselves to the Christian upbringing of the child before bringing him or her to the rite of initiation. In the same way, divorced Catholics are simply being treated as the adults they are when priests or pastoral assistants ask them to reflect prayerfully on their religious commitment, in an atmosphere as free from psychological coercion as possible.

Neither Father Young nor any responsible Catholic is encouraging indifference to the existing legal structure of the Church; they simply recognize that it is always reformable. Young reminded those he worked with that the traditional norm of the Church holds that Catholics who marry outside the Church "cannot receive the Eucharist, because their new 'irregular' second marriage placed them at odds with the Church's teaching and laws on marriage." But his experience was in agreement with that of many bishops, priests, and ordinary practicing Catholics: Many of those contracting such second marriages remain deeply committed to the Church and wish to make such marriages the center of a deeper life of faith. One must be realistic and recognize that there are other divorced—and non-divorced—Catholics who have interiorly broken their ties to their Christian heritage; they should not be encouraged to "play at" being Catholics in order to gain social approval or please their parents. Father Young's approach was to conscientiously advise the "second married" to resolve the status of their marriage through the tribunal which provides them with clear access, after an annulment, to Communion—and, when this is not possible, to "talk over their situation with a priest or other Church pastoral minister who can assist them in making an appropriate decision"; but he concluded that "They alone can decide whether there is any barrier that keeps them from receiving the Eucharist in faith and love."

The Church has the responsibility to resist conformity to the world and to preach the full Gospel, but only a distorted theology and a truncated pastoral policy would countenance the widespread alienation of so many divorced and remarried Catholics—and their absence from the Lord's table to which they have been invited.

Discussion Questions

1. On what grounds should anyone be deprived of pastoral ministry?

2. Is there any way to guarantee that a sacrament is being worthily received?

3. Why are failures to live up to the ideal of Christian marriage treated more harshly in the Church than failures to observe Jesus' counsels in his Sermon on the Mount?

Bibliography

James J. Young, CSP, DIVORCING, BELIEVING, BELONGING. Ramsey, NJ: Paulist, 1984. MINISTERING TO THE DIVORCED CATHOLIC. Ramsey, NJ: Paulist, 1979.

Kevin T. Kelly, DIVORCE AND SECOND MARRIAGE. London: Collins, 1982.

Stephen J. Kelleher, DIVORCE AND REMARRIAGE FOR CATHOLICS. New York: Doubleday, 1973.

32. Sexist Language

Arlene Swidler

*All Catholics have the right to expect that Church documents and
materials will avoid sexist language and that symbols and imagery
of God will not be exclusively masculine.*

Two distinct problems are included under the phrase "sexist language." The first, not particularly Catholic or even religious, is the use
of ambiguous words like *man*, which sometimes refer to males only but
sometimes include women as well. We often find this sort of language in
our hymns: "Sons of God," "Happy the Man," "Faith of Our Fathers,"
"Crown Thy Good With Brotherhood."

Many women, not at all flattered at being lumped under the term
man or *brother*, have pointed out that there are practical effects: If you
ask for a recommendation for "a good man for the job," that's precisely
what you'll get. In the past, directives that *laymen* might undertake certain roles were interpreted in differing ways.

The secular world moved ahead on the issue long ago; Casey and
Swift (below) listed publishers who provide free copies of their own
guidelines for avoiding sexist language and stereotypes.

The second problem is that the language we use to speak of and to
address God has usually been exclusively masculine. For Catholics, who

---

Arlene Swidler is Adjunct Professor of Religious Studies at Villanova
University, Philadelphia, PA.

believe that we humans are made in the image and likeness of God, to speak of God solely in masculine terms is to assert that the human male is more godlike than the female. The practical implications can be seen in attitudes toward the ordination of women. Scholars from the Episcopal, Greek Orthodox and Jewish traditions have all argued that a priest or rabbi represents God, and that a woman in that role is impossible, or at best, confusing.

Clearly the perspective of the Bible is heavily masculine. Yet there are passages which provide a basis for addressing God as Mother as well as Father. One is Dt. 32:18, the Song of Moses: "You forgot the God who writhed in labor pains with you." The translations differ greatly. The Revised Standard Version and the New American Bible both speak of "the God who gave you birth," a feminine image. The Jerusalem Bible, unfortunately, distorts the passage: "unmindful of the God who fathered you."

In the New Testament we find three parallel images in the parables in Luke 15: the good shepherd, the woman who loses a coin, and the father of the prodigal son. Each of these three represents God rejoicing over the recovery of what was lost. That the sex of the woman seeking the coin is not the point of the parable stresses for us that Jesus—and Luke—were so comfortable with the idea of God in female form that they used it without comment.

Within later Christian tradition perhaps the most usable authority is Pope John Paul I, who in his brief pontificate made news by asserting that "God is a father, but he is even more a mother" (National Catholic Reporter, 6 October 1978).

Simply to say that God has feminine or motherly qualities will not suffice. Jesus, although he brooded over Jerusalem in motherly fashion, remains a male, and it is for that reason that the Vatican still holds that women cannot image him and are thus excluded from the priesthood. We must feel free to actually refer to the Divine Creator as *She* as well as *He*, as *Mother* as well as *Father*.

This solution—using a religious vocabulary which is both explicitly feminine and explicitly masculine—seems especially appropriate in prayer and in the liturgy, where Catholics seem to be more comfortable if they use such personal language. An alternative remedy is to avoid all sexual references to God; this style seems preferable in theological discourse. "God shows his power," for example, might become "God shows the divine power," or "God's power is shown. . . ."

Implementing 32 requires dialogue not only with the hierarchy but also with publishers, writers of hymns, preachers. Listening to ourselves will be instructive too.

Discussion Questions

1. What effect does the heavy emphasis on God the Father in our catechetical materials have on our children?

2. Why are some people so opposed to praying to God as both Mother and Father?

3. Try rewriting some of your favorite hymns to eliminate sexist language.

Bibliography

Casey Miller, and Kate Swift, WORDS AND WOMEN. Garden City: Doubleday, 1976. An intelligent and readable introduction to the problems of sexist language, with an excellent chapter on "the language of religion."

Sharon Neufer Emswiler and Thomas Neufer Emswiler, WOMEN AND WORSHIP: A GUIDE TO NON-SEXIST PRAYERS, AND LITURGIES. New York: Harper & Row, 1974. Two Protestant ministers explain the rationale behind non-sexist language, give concrete advice on making changes, and offer sample "liberated" prayers.

Johannes-Baptist Metz, and Edward Schillebeeckx, eds., GOD AS FATHER? CON-CILIUM 143. New York: Seabury, 1981. Essays by seventeen theologians, American and European women and men.

APPENDIX I

Relevant Canons From The

1983 Code Of Canon Law

Canon 208. In virtue of their rebirth in Christ there exists among all the Christian faithful a true equality with regard to dignity and the activity where by all cooperate in the building up of the Body of Christ in accord with each one's own condition and function.

Canon 212:2. The Christian faithful are free to make known their needs, especially spiritual ones, and their desires to the pastors of the Church.

3. In accord with the knowledge, competence and preeminence which they possess, they have the right and even at times a duty to manifest to the sacred pastors their opinion on matters which pertain to the good of the Church, and they have a right to make their opinion known to the other Christian faithful, with due regard for the integrity of faith and morals and reverence toward their pastors, and with consideraiton for the common good and the dignity of persons.

Canon 213. The Christian faithful have the right to receive assistance from the sacred pastors out of the spiritual goods of the Church, especially the word of God and the sacraments.

Canon 214. The Christian faithful have the right to worship God according to the prescriptions of their own rite approved by the legitimate pastors of the Church, and to follow their own form of spiritual life consonant with the teaching of the Church.

Canon 215. The Christain faithful are at liberty freely to found and to govern associations for charitable and religious purposes or for the promotion of the Christian vocation in the world; they are free to hold meetings to pursue these purposes in common.

Canon 216. All the Christian faithful, since they participate in the mission of the Church, have the right to promote or to sustain apostolic action by their own undertakings in accord with each one's state and condition; however, no undertaking shall assume the name Cahtolic unless the consent of competent ecclesiastical authority is given.

Canon 217. The Christian faithful, since they are called by baptism to lead a life in conformity with the teaching of the gospel, have the right to a Christian education by which they will be properly instructed so as to develop the maturity of a human person and at the same time to come to know and live the mystery of salvation.

Canon 218. Those who are engaged in the sacred disciplines enjoy a lawful freedom of inquiry and of prudently expressing their opinions on matters in which they have expertise, while observing due respect for the magisterium of the Church.

Canon 219. All the Christain faithful have the right to be free from any kind of coercion in choosing a state of life.

Canon 220. No one is permitted to damage unlawfully the good reputation which another person enjoys nor to violate the right of another person to protect his or her own privacy.

Canon 221:1. The Christian faithful can legitimately vindicate and defend the rights which they enjoy in the Church before a competent ecclesiastical court in accord with the norm of law.

2. The Christian faithful also have the right, if they are summoned to judgment by competent authority, that they be judged in accord with the prescription of the law to be applied with equity.

3. The Christian faithful have the right not to be punished with canonical penalties except in accord with the norm of the law.

Canon 222:2. The Christian faithful are obliged to promote social justice and, mindful of the precept of the Lord, to assist the poor from their own resources.

Canon 223:1. In exercising their rights the Christian faithful, both as individuals and when gathered in associations, must take account of the common good of the Church and of the rights of others as well as their own duties toward others.

2. In the interest of the common good, ecclesiastical authority has competence to regulate the exercise of the rights which belong to the Christian faithful.

Canon 224. In addition to those obligations and rights which are common to all the Christian faithful and those which are determined in other canons, the lay Christian faithful are bound by the obligations and possess the rights which are enumerated in the canons of this title.

Canon 225:1. Since the laity, like all the Christian faithful, are deputed by God to the apostolate through their baptism and confirmation, they are therefore bound by the general obligations and enjoy the general right to work as individuals or in associations so that the divine message of salvation becomes known and accepted by all persons throughout the world; this obligation has a greater impelling force in those circumstances in which people can hear the gospel and know Christ only through lay persons.

2. Each lay person in accord with his or her condition is bound by a special duty to imbue and perfect the order to temporal affairs with the spirit of the gospel; they thus give witness to Christ in a special way in carrying out those affairs and in exercising secular duties.

Canon 226:2. Because they have given life to their children, parents have a most serious obligation and enjoy the right to educate them; therefore Christian parents are especially to care for the Christian education of their children according to the teaching handed on by the Church.

Canon 227. Lay Christian faithful have the right to have recognized that freedom in the affairs of the earthly city which belongs to all citizens; when they exercise such freedom, however, they are to take care that their actions are imbued with the spirit of the gospel and take into account the doctrine set forth by the magisterium of the Church; but they are to avoid proposing their own opinion as the teaching of the Church in questions which are open to various opinions.

Canon 229:1. Lay persons are bound by the obligation and possess the right to acquire a knowledge of Christian doctrine adapted to their capacity and condition so that they can live in accord with that doctrine, announce it, defend it when necessary, and be enabled to assume their role in exercising the apostolate.

2. Lay persons also possess the right to acquire that deeper knowledge of the sacred sciences which are taught in ecclesiastical universities or faculties or in institutes of religious sciences by attending classes and obtaining academic degrees.

Canon 230:1. Lay men who possess the age and qualifications determined by decree of the conference of bishops can be installed on a stable basis in the ministries of lector and acolyte in accord with the prescribed liturgical rite; the conferral of these mininstries, however, does not confer on these lay men a right to obtain support or remuneration from the Church.

2. Lay persons can fulfill the function of lector during liturgical actions by temporary deputation; likewise, all lay persons can fulfill the functions of commentator or cantor or other functions, in accord with the norm of law.

3. When the necessity of the Church warrants it and when ministers are lacking, lay persons, even if they are not lectors or acolytes, can also supply for certain of their offices, namely, to exercise the ministry of the Word, to preside over liturgical prayers, to confer baptism, and to distribute Holy Communion in accord with the prescriptions of law.

Canon 231:1. Lay persons who devote themselves permanently or temporarily to some special service of the Church are obliged to acquire the appropriate formation which is required to fulfill their function properly and to carry it out conscientiously, zealously, and diligently.

2. With due regard for Canon 230:1, they have a right to a decent remuneration suited to their condition; by such remuneration they should be able to provide decently for their own needs and for those of their family with due regard for the prescriptions of the civil law; they likewise have a right that their pension, social security and health benefits be duly provided.

Canon 274:1. Only clerics can obtain those offices for whose exercise there is required the power of orders or the power of ecclesiastical governance.

Canon 279:1. Even after their ordination to the priesthood clerics are to continue to pursue sacred studies; they are to strive after that solid doctrine which is based upon Sacred Scripture, handed down by their predecessors and commonly accepted by the Church and which is contained especially in the documents of the councils and of the Roman Pontiffs; they are to avoid profane novelties and psuedo-science.

Canon 281:1. When clerics dedicate themselves to the ecclesiastical ministry they deserve a remuneration which is consistent with their condition in accord with the nature of their responsibilities and with the conditions of time and place; this remuneration should enable them to provide for the needs of their own life and for the equitable payment of those whose services they need.

Canon 299:1. The Christian faithful are free, by means of a private agreement made among themselves, to establish associations to attain the aims mentioned in Canon 298:1, with due regard for the prescriptions of Canon 301:1.

Canon 300. No association shall assume the name "Catholic" without the consent of competent ecclesiastical authority, in accord with the norm of Canon 312.

Canon 305. All associations of the Christian faithful are subject to the vigilance of competent ecclesiastical authority, whose duty it is to take care that integrity of faith and morals is preserved in them and to watch lest abuse creep into ecclesiastical discipline; therefore that authority has the right and duty to visit them in accord with the norm of law and the statutes; such associations are also subject to the governance of the same authority according to the prescriptions of the following canons.

Canon 309. Legitimately constituted associations have the right, in accord with the law and the statutes, to issue particular norms respecting the association itself, to hold meetings, to designate moderators, officials, other officers and administrators of goods.

Canon 369. A diocese is a portion of the people of God which is entrusted for pastoral care to a bishop with the cooperation of the presbyterate so that, adhering to its pastor and gathered by him in the Holy Spirit through the gospel and the Eucharist, it constitutes a particular church in which the one, holy, catholic and apostolic Church of Christ is truly present and operative.

Canon 492:1. In each diocese a finance council is to be established by the bishop, over which he himself or his delegate presides, and which is to be composed of at least three members of the Christian faithful truly skilled in financial affairs as well as in civil law, of outstanding integrity and appointed by the bishop.

Canon 515:1. A parish is a definite community of the Christian faithful established on a stable basis within a particular church; the pastoral care of the parish is entrusted to a pastor as its own shepherd under the authority of the diocesan bishop.

Canon 537. Each parish is to have a finance council which is regulated by universal law as well as by norms issued by the diocesan bishop; in this council the Christian faithful, selected according to the same norms, aid the pastor in the administration of parish goods with due regard for the prescription of Canon 532.

Canon 702:1. Those who have legitimately left a religious institute or have been legitimately dismissed from one can request nothing from it for any work done in it.

2. The institute however is to observe equity and evangelical charity toward the member who is separated from it.

Canon 747:1. The Church, to whom Christ the Lord entrusted the deposit of faith so that, assisted by the Holy Spirit, it might reverently safeguard revealed truth, more closely examine it and faithfully proclaim and expound it, has the innate duty and right to preach the gospel to all nations, independent of any human power whatever, using the means of social communication proper to it.

Canon 748:1. All persons are bound to seek the truth in matters concerning God and God's Church; by divine law they also are obliged and have the right to embrace and to observe that truth which they have recognized.

Canon 749:1. The Supreme Pontiff, in virtue of his office, possesses infallible teaching authority when, as supreme pastor and teacher of all the faithful, whose task is to confirm his fellow believers in the faith, he proclaims with a definitive act that a doctrine of faith or morals is to be held as such.

Canon 750. All that is contained in the written word of God or in tradition, that is, in the one deposit of faith entrusted to the Church and also proposed as divinely revealed either by the solemn magisterium of the Church or by its ordinary and universal magisterium, must be believed with divine and catholic faith; it is manifested by the common adherence of the Christian faithful under the leadership of the sacred magisterium; therefore, all are bound to avoid any doctrines whatever which are contrary to these truths.

Canon 752. A religious respect of intellect and will, even if not the assent of faith, is to be paid to the teaching which the Supreme Pontiff or the college of bishops enuntiate on faith or morals when they exercise the authentic magisterium even if they do not intend to proclaim it with a definitive act; therefore the Christian faithful are to take care to avoid whatever is not in harmony with that teaching.

Canon 753. Although they do not enjoy infallible teaching authority, the bishops in communion with the head and members of the college, whether as individuals or gathered in conferences of bishops or in particular councils, are authentic teachers and instructors of the faith for the faithful entrusted to their care; the faithful must adhere to the authentic teaching of their own bishops with a sense of religious respect.

Canon 754. All the Christian faithful are obliged to observe the constitutions and decrees which the legitimate authority of the Church issues in order to propose doctrine and proscribe erroneous opinions; this is especially true of the constitutions and decrees issued by the Roman Pontiff or the college of bishops.

Canon 774:1. Under the supervision of legitimate ecclesiastical authority this concern for catechesis pertains to all the members of the Church in proportion to each one's role.

Canon 794:1. The duty and right of educating belongs in a unique way to the Church which has been divinely entrusted with the mission to assist men and women so that they can arrive at the fullness of the Christian life.

Canon 810. It is the responsibility of the authority who is competent in accord with the statues to provide for the appointment of teachers to Catholic universities who besides their scientific and pedagogical suitability are also outstanding in their integrity of doctrine and probity of life; when those requisite qualities are lacking they are to be removed from their positions in accord with the procedure set forth in the statutes.

Canon 812. It is necessary that those who teach theological disciplines in any institute of higher studies have a mandate from the competent ecclesiastical authority.

Canon 819. Insofar as the good of a diocese, a religious institute or indeed the universal Church itself requires it, diocesan bishops or the competent superiors of institutes must send to ecclesiastical universities or faculties young people, clerics and members who are outstanding for their character, virtue and talent.

Canon 843:1. The sacred ministers can not refuse the sacraments to those who ask for them at appropriate times, are properly disposed and are not prohibited by law from receiving them.

Canon 1024. Only a baptized male validly receives sacred ordination.

Canon 1151. Spouses have the duty and the right to preserve conjugal living unless a legitimate cause excuses them.

Canon 1287:2. Administrators are to render an account to the faithful concerning the goods offered by the faithful to the Church, according to norms to be determined by particular law.

APPENDIX II

The Universal Declaration of Human Rights of the United Nations

Article 1. All human beings are born free and equal in dignity and rights. They are endowed with reason and conscience and should act toward one another in a spirit of brotherhood.

Article 2. Everyone is entitled to all the rights and freedoms set forth in this Declaration, without distinction of any kind, such as race, colour, sex, language, religion, political or other opinion, national or social origin, property, birth or other status. Furthermore, no distinction shall be made on the basis of the political, jurisdictional or international status of the country or territory to which a person belongs, whether it be independent, trust, non-self-governing or under any other limitation of sovereignty.

Article 3. Everyone has the right to life, liberty and security of person.

Article 4. No one shall be held in slavery or servitude; slavery and the slave trade shall be prohibited in all their forms.

176 A Catholic Bill of Rights

Article 5. No one shall be subjected to torture or to cruel, inhuman or degrading treatment or punishment.

Article 6. Everyone has the right to a recognition everywhere as a person before the law.

Article 7. All are equal before the law and are entitled without any discrimination to equal protection of the law. All are entitled to equal protection against any discrimination in violation of this Declaration and against any incitement to such discrimination.

Article 8. Everyone has the right to an effective remedy by the competent national tribunal for acts violating the fundamental rights granted him by the constitution or by law.

Article 9. No one shall be subjected to arbitrary arrest, detention or exile.

Article 10. Everyone is entitled in full equality to a fair and public hearing by an independent and impartial tribunal, in the determination of his rights and obligations and of any criminal charge against him.

Article 11. Everyone charged with a penal offence has the right to be presumed innocent until proved guilty according to law in a public trial at which he has had all the guarantees necessary for his defence. (2) No one shall be held guilty of any penal offence on account of any act or omission which did not constitute a penal offence, under national or international law, at the time when it was committed. Nor shall a heavier penalty be imposed than the one that was applicable at the time the penal offence was committed.

Article 12. No one shall be subjected to arbitrary interference with his privacy, family, home or correspondence, not to attacks upon his honour and reputation. Everyone has the right to the protection of the law against such interference or attacks.

Article 13. (1) Everyone has the right to freedom of movement and residence within the borders of each state. (2) Everyone has the right to leave any country, including his own, and to return to his country.

Article 14. (1) Everyone has the right to seek and to enjoy in other countries asylum from persecution. (2) This right may not be invoked in the case of prosecutions genuinely arising from non-political crimes or from acts contrary to the purposes and principles of the United Nations.

Article 15. (1) Everyone has the right to a nationality. (2) No one shall be aribitrarily deprived of his nationality nor denied the right to change his nationality.

Article 16. (1) Men and women of full age, without any limitation due to race, nationality or religion, have the right to marry and to found a family. They are entitled to equal rights as to marriage, during marriage and at its dissolution. (2) Marriage shall be entered into only with the free and full consent of the intending spouses. (3) The family is the natural and fundamental group unit of society and is entitled to protection by society and the state.

Article 17. (1) Everyone has the right to own property alone as well as in association with others. (2) No one shall be arbitrarily deprived of his property.

Article 18. Everyone has the right to freedom of thought, conscience and religion; this right includes freedom to change his religion or belief, and freedom, either alone or in community with others and in public or private, to manifest his religion or belief in teaching, practice, worship and observance.

Article 19. Everyone has the right to freedom of opinion and expression; this right includes freedom to hold opinions without interference and to seek, receive and impart information and ideas through any media, regardless of frontiers.

Article 20. (1) Everyone has the right to freedom of peaceful assembly and association. (2) No one may be compelled to belong to an association.

Article 21. (1) Everyone has the right to take part in the government of his country, directly or through freely chosen representatives. (2) Everyone has the right of equal access to public service in his country. (3) The will of the people shall be the basis of the authority of government; this will shall be expressed in periodic and genuine elections which shall be by universal and equal suffrage and shall be held by secret vote or by equivalent free voting procedures.

Article 22. Everyone, as member of a society, has the right to social security and is entitled to realization, through national effort and international cooperation and in accordance with the organization and resources of each State, of the economic, social and cultural rights indepensable for his dignity and the free development of his personality.

Article 23. (1) Everyone has the right to work, to free choice of employment, to just and favourable conditions of work and to protection against unemployment. (2) Everyone, without any discrimination, has the right to equal pay for equal work. (3) Everyone who works has the right to just and favourable remuneration ensuring for himself and his family an existence worthy of human dignity, and supplemented, if necessary, by other means of social protection. (4) Everyone has the right to form and to join trade unions for the protection of his interests.

Article 24. Everyone has the right to rest and leisure, including reasonable limitation of working hours and periodic holidays with pay.

Article 25. (1) Everyone has the right to a standard of living adequate for the health and well-being of himself and of his family, including food, clothing, housing and medical care and necessary social services. and the right to security in the event of unemployment, sickness, disability, widowhood, old age or other lack of livelihood in circumstances beyond his control. (2) Motherhood and childhood are entitled to special care and assistance. All children, whether born in or out of wedlock, shall enjoy the same protection.

Article 26. (1) Everyone has the right to education. Education shall be free, at least in the elementary and fundamental stages. Elementary education shall be compulsory. Technical and professional education shall be made generally available and higher education shall be equally accessible to all on the basis of merit. (2) Education shall be directed to the full development of the human personality and to the strengthening of respect for human rights and fundamental freedoms. It shall promote understanding, tolerance and friendship among all nations, racial or religious groups, and shall further the activities of the United Nations for the maintenance of peace. (3) Parents have a prior right to choose the kind of education that shall be given to their children.

Article 27. (1) Everyone has the right freely to participate in the cultural life of the community, to enjoy the arts and to share in scientific advancement and its benefits. (2) Everyone has the right to the protection of the moral and material interests resulting from any scientific, literary or artistic production of which he is the author.

Article 28. Everyone is entitled to a social and international order in which the rights and freedoms set forth in this Declaration can be fully realized.

Article 29. (1) Everyone has duties to the community in which alone the free and full development of his personality is possible. (2) In the exercise of his rights and freedoms, everyone shall be subject only to such limitations as are determined by law solely for purpose of securing due recognition and respect for the rights and freedoms of others and of meeting the just requirements of morality, public order and the general welfare in a democratic society. (3) These rights and freedoms may in no case be exercised contrary to the purposes and principles of the United Nations.

Article 30. Nothing in this Declaration may be interpreted as implying for any State, group or person any right to engage in any activity or to perform any act aimed at the destruction of any of the rights and freedoms set forth herein.

APPENDIX III
Dissent and Dialogue in the Church

All Catholics have the right to express publicly their dissent in regard to decisions made by Church authorities.

Catholic teachers of theology have a right to responsible academic freedom. The acceptability of their teaching is to be judged in dialogue with their peers, keeping in mind the legitimacy of responsible dissent and pluralism of belief.

—Charter of the Rights of Catholics in the Church, nos. 8, 20.

"The right to responsible dissent" refers to public dissent from noninfallible teachings of the official Church. Infallible statements are those which are explicitly declared to be so. The Association for the Rights of Catholics in the Church (ARCC) bases both rights cited on a Vatican II collegial understanding of the Church. This understanding sees the *whole* Church, the entire people of God, as a learning and teaching Church. This is in contrast to a relatively recent pre-Vatican II (but not truly traditional) ecclesiology, which saw the pope and bishops as the sole teachers and the rest of the faithful as uncritical learners. In this model of the Church any kind of dissent was in effect ruled out, whether a teaching was proposed as infallible or not.

The post-Vatican II Code of Canon Law adverts to the collegial model of the church both for the faithful in general and for teachers of theology in particular: "The Christian faithful...have the right and even at times a duty to manifest to the sacred pastors their opinion on matters which pertain to the good of the Church, and they have a right to make their opinion known to the other Christian faithful" (Canon 212,3): "Those who are engaged in the sacred disciplines enjoy a lawful freedom of enquiry and of prudently expressing their opinions on matters in which they have expertise, while observing a due respect for the magisterium of the Church" (Canon 218).

ARCC is convinced that there are times when public dissent from non-infallible teaching is a *duty* for a Catholic, and especially for a theologian. Such public dissent will be motivated by a desire to deepen the Church's understanding of its teachings and, indeed, will have proceeded from the notion that the teaching in place enjoys the presumption of truth. Dissent from that teaching will flow from careful and prayerful study and dialogue. Such dissent will be a positive contribution to the Church's self-understanding.

In fact, Church history provides many examples of the official Church's ultimately incorporating into its body of teaching what were originally dissenting opinions: thus, St. Paul's dissenting views were adopted over St. Peter's; St. Thomas Aquinas's books, burned by bishops, became a bulwark of Catholic teaching; Vatican II paid heed to those theologians who had dissented from the traditional teaching on religious liberty and radically reversed that teaching.

An objection to public dissent is that it supposedly gives scandal to the faithful. ARCC contends, however, that if giving scandal means harming the faithful by leading them astray, then scandal is given indeed not when dissent is expressed publicly, but when harmful teachings are not corrected as a result of the public dialogue arising out of dissent. Thus, in 1968, in speaking of the possibility of "licit theological dissent," the U.S. bishops stated: "The expression of theological dissent is in order only if the reasons are serious and well-founded, if the manner of dissent does not question or impugn the teaching authority of the Church, and is such as not to give scandal." The previous year in a pastoral letter the Bishops of Germany had written: "To safeguard the real substance of the faith, the Church must give doctrinal instructions which have a certain degree of obligation, but, not being definitions of faith,

182 A Catholic Bill of Rights

have a certain provisional character, even to the extent of possible error."

ARCC by no means wishes to "impugn the teaching authority of the Church." ARCC recognizes the need for authoritative Church proclamations on matters of faith and morals. However, ARCC does reject that interpretation of Canon 752 that claims that the same type of religious assent must be given to both infallible and non-infallible statements. If this were so, then why make a distinction at all between the two types of statements? Everything, then, in effect would be infallible. Is this traditional Church teaching? If not, then non-infallible teachings are by definition, fallible, and, thus possibly reformable. How else could they be reformed, then, unless public dissent and dialogue are allowed?

Even the Congregation of the Doctrine of the Faith in its 1973 decree *Mysterium ecclesiae* states that the "conceptions" by which Church teaching is expressed are changeable: "Even though the truths which the Church intends to teach through her dogmatic formulas are distinct from the changeable conceptions of a given epoch and can be expressed without them; nevertheless it can sometimes happen that these truths may be enunciated by the sacred magisterium in terms that bear traces of those conceptions." ARCC asks: How can these "conceptions" be changed unless someone points out that they might be improved and may even be defective?

Pope John Paul II himself encouraged both the faithful in public dissent and theologians in their invaluable service done in freedom: In 1969, then Archbishop of Cracow, he said, "Conformity means death for any community. A loyal opposition is a necessity in any community." A decade later, as pope, he declared: "The Church needs her theologians particularly in this time and age... . We desire to listen to you and we are eager to receive the valued assistance of your responsible scholarship... . We will never tire of insisting on the eminent role of the university...a place of scientific research, constantly updating its methods and working instruments... *in freedom of investigation.*"

ARCC claims that among the "signs of the times" the Church must pay attention to are that spirit of open enquiry and dialogue, of academic freedom, of intellectual integrity and freedom of conscience that are so highly valued in the contemporary world. Indeed, ARCC would argue that Vatican II's Declaration on Religious Liberty enshrines those values, values which undergird the right to public dissent in the Church. Thus: "Nobody is forced to act against his convictions in religious matters in private or in public.... Truth can impose itself on the mind of man only in virtue of its own truth.... The search for truth (should be carried out) by free enquiry...and dialogue.... Man is bound to follow his conscience faithfully in all his activity.... He must not be forced to act contrary to his conscience especially in religious matters."

Catholic Christianity is a living faith, not a dead imitation of a past which no longer exists. Catholic theology is a contemporary reflection in today's thought categories on present questions and problems about what it means to think and live as a Catholic Christian in this concrete world. To parrot the past is to pervert it. To be a Christian means to make what Jesus thought, taught and wrought understandable and applicable in today's language and life. Christian life and theology must be something dynamic, not dead, and therefore at its heart there must be deliberation, dissent, dialogue, decision—which leads to further deliberation, dissent...

The function of the Congregation of the Doctrine of Faith, therefore, ought not be to put a stop to deliberation, dissent and dialogue, but instead precisely to encourage, promote and direct it in the most creative possible channels.

Indeed, even the pope and the Vatican have stressed the absolute necessity of dialogue—which presupposes dissent—and sketched out how it should be conducted. Pope Paul VI in his first encyclical, *Ecclesiam suam* (1964), wrote that dialogue "is demanded nowadays...it is demanded by the dynamic course of action which is changing the face of modern society. It is demanded by the...maturity man has reached in this day and age." Then in 1968, the Vatican declared that "the willingness to engage in dialogue is the measure and strength of that general renewal which must be carried out in the Church, which *implies a still greater appreciation of liberty...* . Doctrinal dialogue should be initiated with courage and sincerity, *with the greatest freedom*...recognizing the truth everywhere, even if the truth demolishes one so that one is forced to reconsider one's own position... . Therefore *the liberty of the participants* must be ensured by law and reverenced in practice" (*Humane personae dignitatem*).

To paraphrase Gamaliel (Acts 5:36-39): If the dissenter is in error, nothing will come of it: but if the dissenter is showing us a truth we have not seen, God is with the dissenter, and the truth will prevail. Not only that, but "the truth will set us free."

APPENDIX IV
Guidelines for Conflict Resolution in the Church

Many Catholics are not aware that, as members of the Church, they have a broad range of rights and the freedom necessary to pursue their religious responsibilities and initiatives. These rights and freedoms are guaranteed by the law and doctrine of the Church and they can be protected and vindicated by means of procedures available for resolving conflicts. *Due Process* is the term used for these procedures, both formal and informal. Because justice is "love's absolute minimum," Christians do a real service to the Church when they try to find truly just solutions to disputes by making use of *Due Process*. When conflicts are thus identified and resolved, the result often extends beyond the immediate concerns of the parties and can help administrators improve procedures and policies.

When conflict arises, what can you do? The following are some options that are available within the framework of the law and discipline of the Church. Other options, beyond the scope of *Due Process*, are also available to the Christian community. These lie in the area of political action and public opinion. They will be discussed in other contexts.

Informal Conciliation Measures

1. Take time to clarify what is happening and to sort out the issues. Gather your support network together and conjointly explore all the dimensions of the dispute. Think the matter through to a position of your own for which you can take responsiblity.

2. In a spirit of peacemaking, try to resolve the dispute directly with the other person(s) who are involved. Try to avoid threats and hardening of positions. Stop the discussion short of full dispute if you can so that some avenue to return to the discussion remains open.

3. If the above attempt fails, seek consultation with the Parish Council, the pastor, or any existing group at the parish level that exercises some decision-making authority. If the dispute is with the pastor or bishop, identify some person(s) at the parish or diocesan level, who you know to be fair and knowledgeable, and ask them to accompany you.

4. If the matter still cannot be resolved, offer to enter into an informal process of mediation/conciliation with a person neutral to the dispute who can be fair and who is also acceptable to authority.

5. If you are unable to resolve the dispute through informal mediation/conciliation measures, move to the implementation of formal *Due Process* procedures at the diocesan level.

Formal Conciliation/Arbitration Measures

1. Call the diocesan office and ask if there is a Board of Conciliation/Arbitration or other agency of *Due Process*. Write to the Chairperson of the Board. If there is no Board established in your diocese, ask for the procedures for conciliation/arbitration in the diocese. Follow the procedures, seeking competent consultation with a canon lawyer or knowledgeable person who can advise you as you proceed. ARCC can try to help you find competent assistance if you write to us.

2. If the parties to the disputes do not consent to conciliation, write directly to the diocesan bishop. If the bishop is a party to the dispute, or if he is unresponsive, write to the Chair of the National Conference of Catholic Bishops' Committee on Conciliation and Arbitration, 1312 Massachusetts Avenue, N.W., Washington, DC 20005.

3. If you do not gain the cooperation of the diocesan structures in initiating *Due Process,* move outside the diocesan community to other na-

tional groups (like *ARCC* or *Catholics Speak Out*) to apply pressure. At the same time, seek consultation from civil authority about the appropriateness of your case with regard to civil procedures.

Remember...

Your task is to get the dispute resolved at the *earliest possible stage*, at the point *nearest to the dispute*, by *those* who are *most affected*.

Bureaucratic structures that are distant from the point of the dispute (e.g., Rome) are responsive to extra community pressure such as the press. However, they also have a tendency to overreact to factors external to the dispute, and this can distort the situation and contribute to a hardening of positions.

Formal Judicial Remedies

1. Canon law provides for the judicial redress of violations of the law of the Church. It also stipulates that legal advice and counsel be made available to those needing it. If the conflict in question involves the violation of a law of the Church, contact the Promoter of Justice of your diocese or one of the officially appointed advocates of the diocese. ARCC will assist you in this if you need help.

2. The judicial approach does not preclude non-judicial arbitration or conciliation; it may, in fact, facilitate it. This approach would usually find canonical advice helpful. Contact a canon lawyer or ARCC for assistance.

ARCC, P.O. Box 912, Delran, NJ 08075. Tel. (609) 764-9266.

Prepared by Margaret Cotroneo and Sidney Callahan, in consultation with James Coriden.